Tennessee Test Power

Grade 4

Photo Credits:

30 ©sambrogio/Getty Images; 100 ©KidStock/Blend Images/Getty Images; 172 ©ieriss/JupiterImages/Getty Images; 127 ©D. Hurst/Alamy.

Copyright © by Houghton Mifflin Harcourt Publishing Company

Printed in the U.S.A.

ISBN 978-0-547-93884-4

3 4 5 6 7 8 9 10   0982   24 23 19 18 17 16 15 14 13

4500A00350   BCDEFG

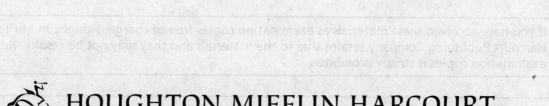

HOUGHTON MIFFLIN HARCOURT

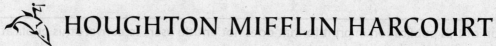

Contents

Introduction

What Is the *Tennessee Test Power* Book?

The *Tennessee Test Power* book is a workbook that helps you prepare to take the TCAP and tests of the Common Core State Standards. The questions in these tests are based on the skills you learn in school.

The Reading/Language Arts Test in this book tests your reading and language arts skills. For some questions, you will read passages and answer questions about them. For other questions, you will read writing and answer questions about how to make the writing better. The Writing Test in this book has you write a response to a prompt. Constructed Response Practice has you read stories and articles and write answers to questions about them.

How to Use this Book

This book includes reading, language arts, and writing lessons. The reading lessons review skills that help you understand different kinds of reading material. The language arts and writing lessons review the steps in the writing process.

You will get the most out of the reading experience if you ask yourself questions as you read:

- What is the passage mostly about?
- What do I already know about this topic?
- Is the passage making sense to me?
- Which parts do I need to reread?
- What can I do to understand words that I do not know?
- What did I learn from the passage?

You will get the most out of the language arts and writing experience if you do the following:

- Think about a plan before you write.
- Make a first try at the writing.
- Think about ways to make the writing better.
- Make changes to improve the writing.
- Think about the best sources to use to research a topic.

Learning to read and write well is like learning to ride a bike. The more you practice, the easier it becomes. Before you know it, you are riding with ease. So, let's hop on and get started!

Name _____ Date _____

Story Structure

Skill Overview

The story *Because of Winn-Dixie* takes place in a small town in Florida, probably during the 1960s. It is important that the story is set there and then so that Opal can have the experiences that she does.

The **setting** of a story is the time and place in which the story happens. To identify the setting of a story, ask yourself these questions:

- Where do events in the story happen?
- When do events in the story happen?

Thinking carefully about a story's setting can help you understand why events in the story happen the way they do. Suppose you read a story about a brother and sister who spend the night in a campground. The fact that the children sleep in the woods at night will affect the events and characters in the story.

The **plot** is the story line, or the events that happen. The events in one part of a story influence what happens later. A careful reading of the plot will help you identify which events in one part affect the events in a later part. The plot also helps you understand the conflict, or main problem, in the story and how the characters try to solve the conflict. The way the problem is solved is called the resolution or solution.

When you read a story, asking the following questions will help you understand the plot:

- How is the problem finally solved?
- How does the character try to solve the problem?
- How do events in the story influence other events?
- What is an important problem for a character in the story?

GO ON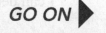

Skill Practice

Directions   Read the folktale. Then answer Numbers 1 through 4.

The Golden Reed Pipe

(A Folktale from China)

1   Long ago in China, there lived a woman and her daughter. The daughter was called Little Red because she always wore red clothing.

> **TIP**
>
> Folktales are stories passed along by word of mouth.

2   One day, Little Red and her mother were plowing and sowing the fields. There was a fierce wind, and then a dragon swooped down! He grabbed Little Red and carried her away. Her mother heard Little Red's voice crying:

Oh mother, oh mother, as dear as can be,

My brother, my brother will rescue me!

> **TIP**
>
> Where does the folktale take place? Think about why the location might be important.

3   The poor mother did not know what to think. She had no son, so Little Red had no brother. The woman was upset as she walked home and did not see the large tree. Her hair became tangled in the trees branches which she noticed had bright red berries. After she untangled herself, she saw a lost little boy under the tree. She brought the boy to live with her and named him Redberry.

4   Redberry was outside one day when he heard a crow cry:

You have a sister out there, out there!

Save her from the dragon's lair!

5   Redberry had no idea he had a sister! He ran to his mother, who told him about Little Red and what had happened. The boy was so angry at the dragon that he set out to rescue his sister. He walked for miles and miles in search of the dragon's lair. Then he came to a large rock that was blocking his way. He rolled the rock away and found a shiny golden reed pipe.

> **TIP**
>
> Stop every few paragraphs to summarize the main events that have happened. Decide if those paragraphs tell about the main problem, or conflict, in the story.

6   When Redberry blew on the pipe, he saw movement out of the corner of his eye. Then he realized that all the frogs and other creatures were dancing. The faster he played the tune, the faster they danced.

7   "Aha!" cried Redberry. "I know just what to do! Now I can deal with the dragon!"

8   When he came to the dragon's cave, he saw a girl dressed in red and knew it was his sister. He also saw a dragon. The dragon was scarier than Redberry expected.

9   Redberry blew on the pipe, and the dragon began to dance. The faster Redberry played, the faster the dragon danced. At last the dragon cried:

I'll send her home

If you leave me alone!

10   Redberry knew better than to believe a dragon. He led Little Red and the dragon away from the cave. He kept on playing until they came to the sea. With a splash, the dragon fell in! Then the sister and brother returned home hand-in-hand. They both came to their mother, who cried with joy.

> **TIP**
>
> To figure out how the conflict is resolved, ask yourself, "How do things turn out for the characters?"

1   **How can you tell that this is a folktale and not realistic fiction?**

_____

_____

_____

_____

2   **What is the <u>main</u> problem the woman and Redberry face in the folktale?**

_____

_____

_____

_____

GO ON ▶

3 Think about how the author organized information in the folktale.

Complete the timeline with **one** detail from the folktale.

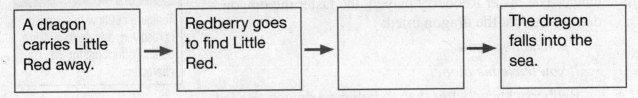

| A dragon carries Little Red away. | → | Redberry goes to find Little Red. | → | | → | The dragon falls into the sea. |

Explain why this detail accurately completes the timeline.

_____

_____

_____

_____

_____

4 How is the problem in the folktale resolved? Give **two** details from the folktale to support your answer.

_____

_____

_____

_____

_____

STOP

Author's Purpose

Skill Overview

In the selection *My Brother Martin,* Dr. Martin Luther King Jr.'s sister reflects on growing up with Dr. King. Her purposes for writing are to describe her experiences and to inform readers about Dr. King.

Authors write for different **purposes**, or reasons. Some purposes that authors have for writing are to describe, to entertain, to explain, to inform, and to persuade. An author often has one clear purpose. Other times an author writes for more than one purpose.

Authors do not usually state why they are writing. It is up to the reader to figure it out, using clues in the selection. Read the chart below to learn more about identifying an author's purpose.

Author's Purpose	Features of the Reading Selection	Examples
To describe	Words that tell how things look, sound, smell, or taste	Essay, letter, magazine article, poem
To entertain	Tells about characters or people and the events in their lives May make readers feel happy, scared, or sad	Play, poem, story
To explain	Gives directions Explains how something works or why something happens	Directions, magazine article, newspaper article
To inform	Gives facts and information	Report, newspaper article, magazine article
To persuade	Tries to get reader to agree with the author Gives beliefs and opinions	Advertisement, book review, letter

GO ON ▶

Name _____ Date _____

Skill Practice

Directions   Read the article. Then answer Numbers 1 through 4.

Land of Fire and Ice

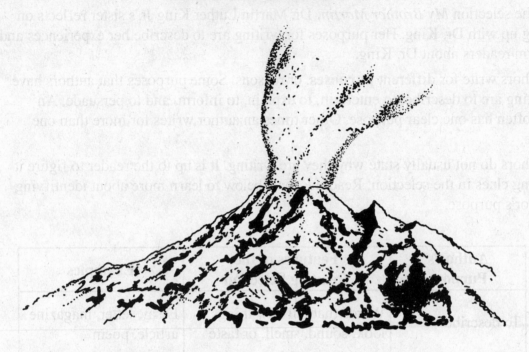

1   Would you like to visit a land where you can see things that are both very hot and very cold? Iceland is a country that has both volcanoes and glaciers. That is why the country is called the "Land of Fire and Ice."

2   Iceland is about the size of the state of Virginia. Still, it has more hot springs and volcanoes than any other country in the world. There are about 200 volcanoes, which makes Iceland one of the busiest volcano areas on the Earth. A volcano erupts in this tiny area about every five years! In 1963, a volcano erupted and made a brand new island. Within four years, because of more eruptions, this island grew to an area of 1 square mile. The island soon rose to more than 560 feet above sea level.

3   Glaciers are another part of Iceland. Glaciers are large, slow-moving masses of ice and snow. Some of the largest glaciers in the world are in Iceland, and much of Iceland is covered with glaciers. In fact, more than 10 percent of Iceland is covered with glaciers. Only Antarctica and Greenland have bigger ones.

> **TIP**
>
> An author usually has one main purpose for writing. As you read, look for clues to decide whether the author wants to describe, entertain, explain, inform, or persuade.

> **TIP**
>
> This article includes many facts. Think about how giving facts relates to the author's purpose.

Name _____ Date _____

4   Iceland lies just below the Arctic Circle. It is warmer, though, than you might think. The waters of the Gulf Stream in the Atlantic Ocean keep Iceland warm. The average July temperature is a very comfortable 51°F. Of course, in winter Iceland gets much colder.

> **TIP**
> To figure out the author's main purpose, ask yourself, "What is the author telling me and why?"

5   Only about 300,000 people live in Iceland. The population is about the same as Knoxville, Tennessee. Most people live in Reykjavik, the capital. They still speak the same basic language as the Vikings who first settled the island. The Vikings, who journeyed by boat from Scandinavia, began settling in Iceland more than a thousand years ago.

6   Icelanders enjoy nature activities. The beautiful and interesting geography attracts visitors who like the outdoors. For all people who enjoy nature at the extreme, Iceland is a paradise of fire and ice.

> **TIP**
> In this paragraph, the author gives an opinion and wants the reader to agree.

1   **What is the most likely reason the author wrote this article?**

   A   to explain how to travel to Iceland

   B   to inform readers about Iceland's geography

   C   to persuade readers that Iceland is very cold

   D   to entertain readers with stories about Iceland

> **TIP**
> Thinking about why someone would want to read this article can help you understand the author's purpose.

1 Ⓐ Ⓑ Ⓒ Ⓓ   GO ON ▶

Name _____ Date _____

2 Which clues in the article **best** help you identify the author's purpose?

   F facts about Iceland

   G stories about the Icelandic people

   H details about how Iceland sounds and smells

   J explanations about how volcanoes and glaciers form

> **TIP**
>
> Look for details, such as facts (inform), sensory details (describe), opinions (persuade), or feeling words (entertain) that suggest why the author wrote the article.

3 Why do you think the author **most likely** chose the title "Land of Fire and Ice" for this article?

   A to frighten and excite readers

   B to explain how Iceland got its name

   C to prevent readers from visiting Iceland

   D to stress Iceland's most interesting features

> **TIP**
>
> The title can help you understand why the author wrote the article.

4 What is the **main** purpose of Paragraph 3?

   F to inform readers about glaciers in Iceland

   G to entertain readers with stories about glaciers

   H to explain why Iceland is covered with glaciers

   J to persuade readers that Iceland has the best glaciers

> **TIP**
>
> Paragraph 3 gives facts about Iceland's glaciers. Think about why the author gives facts instead of opinions or detailed descriptions.

2 Ⓕ Ⓖ Ⓗ Ⓙ
3 Ⓐ Ⓑ Ⓒ Ⓓ
4 Ⓕ Ⓖ Ⓗ Ⓙ

STOP

Cause and Effect

Skill Overview

The selection *My Librarian Is a Camel* tells about the different ways that people deliver books to children living in the world's most faraway places. These moving libraries have a wonderful effect on the children they serve. They deliver happiness along with the books, and they get the children excited about reading.

Authors can connect ideas or events by using cause and effect. A **cause** is a reason that something happens. An **effect** is what happens as a result of the cause.

CAUSE ⟶ EFFECT

To understand cause and effect, ask yourself what happened (effect) and why it happened (cause). As you read, look for words and phrases that might signal a cause-and-effect pattern. These words include <u>as a result</u>, <u>because</u>, <u>since</u>, <u>so</u>, and <u>therefore</u>.

Sometimes an author first explains what happened (effect) and then explains why it happened (cause). Other times the author tells about the cause and then the effect. In some stories, an event can be both an effect of something that has happened and a cause of something else that will happen. Then the series of causes and effects is like a game of tag.

Cause	Effect/Cause	Effect
Ana tags Josh.	Josh is *It*.	Josh tags Ben.

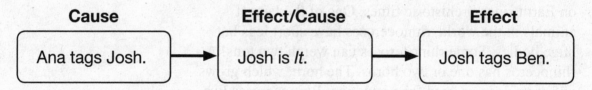

Sometimes a cause can have more than one effect.

A drought, or lack of rain (cause), can cause grass to turn brown, ponds to dry up, and crops to not grow (effects).

Sometimes an effect has more than one cause.

The school fair was a great success (effect) because the food was delicious, there were many new games and prizes, and more people than ever showed up (causes).

GO ON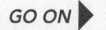

Name _____ Date _____

Skill Practice

Directions Read the article. Then answer Numbers 1 through 4.

Two Endangered Animals

1   Around the world, more than a thousand animals are endangered. If an animal is endangered, it may soon become extinct. There are two animals that scientists fear are disappearing quickly. These animals are the rhinoceros and the giant panda. The threat to these animals grows larger every day, and the time to save them is running out. Extinction is not reversible.

2   A major threat to these endangered animals is the loss of habitat. A habitat is the area in which an animal lives. Habitats are being changed or damaged worldwide. As a result of losing their habitats, animals can no longer find food or places to live. Hunting and poaching also threaten endangered animals. Poachers are those who kill an animal illegally. They may kill it for sport or for parts of its body.

The Rhinoceros in Danger

3   The rhinoceros is an amazing animal. It has lived on Earth since prehistoric times. One of the largest animals in the world, rhinoceroses have short legs but huge bodies. Some rhinoceroses can weigh two tons! A rhinoceros has one or two horns. The horn, which grows out of its nose, is used for protection. Rhinoceroses live in Africa and southeastern Asia.

4   The rhinoceros has nearly disappeared for many reasons. First, since more people are living on its land, the rhinoceros is losing its natural habitat. Another reason is that many people in Asia use the rhinoceros horn for medicine. As a result, poachers kill rhinoceroses just for their horns.

TIP

Remember that a cause tells why something happens and an effect tells what happens.

TIP

To figure out cause-and-effect patterns, draw a diagram with arrows to show how the causes connect to the effects.

TIP

Look for signal words such as <u>because</u>, <u>as a result</u>, <u>since</u>, and <u>so</u> to identify cause-and-effect relationships.

Saving the Rhinoceros

5   Many countries are working as fast as possible to save the rhinoceros. Countries have laws making it illegal to hunt the rhinoceros. Some countries have areas of land in which the rhinoceros's habitat is protected. For instance, most rhinoceroses in Zimbabwe have been moved to nature preserves that are guarded and surrounded by high fences.

Giant Pandas at Risk

6   Giant pandas live in China. They live on high mountain slopes and eat bamboo. These cute black-and-white animals look like giant teddy bears. They can grow to be 5 or 6 feet tall and can weigh 200 to 300 pounds.

7   Like the rhinoceros, the giant panda is facing several real dangers that may cause it to become extinct. First, many of the forests in which giant pandas once lived have been cut down for farming and lumber. Therefore, many giant pandas live without shelter. Second, some bamboo forests aren't growing because of lack of rain. This often causes giant pandas to starve. Finally, because the fur of the giant panda is highly valued, poachers are killing giant pandas for their fur.

> **TIP**
>
> In some cases, an effect may have several causes. Look for words that identify several causes of one effect, such as first and second.

Protecting the Giant Panda

8   The Chinese government has set aside protected land for giant pandas. However, unlike the rhinoceros, the giant panda needs a large area of land on which to live. This is because the giant panda needs massive amounts of bamboo to survive.

9   For the rhinoceros and the giant panda, not much time is left. There are fewer places for them to live. Fortunately, scientists are continuing to work with countries to find solutions to these problems.

GO ON ▶

1   **According to the article, the rhinoceros is in danger of extinction because**

   A   it has many natural predators.

   B   it is hunted by poachers and is losing its natural habitat.

   C   it can no longer grow horns to protect itself.

   D   the giant panda is taking its land.

> **TIP**
>
> Reread Paragraph 4. Which of these matches the causes in the article?

2   **According to the article, what is an effect of the giant panda becoming endangered?**

   F   More and more people are hunting the giant panda for its fur.

   G   It doesn't have enough bamboo to eat.

   H   The Chinese government has set aside land for the giant panda.

   J   It is losing its habitat.

3   **What happens when an animal becomes extinct?**

   A   The animal is gone from the Earth forever.

   B   The animal can be brought back once its habitat is restored.

   C   The animal becomes endangered.

   D   Hunters can continue to hunt the animal.

> **TIP**
>
> Not all causes and effects are directly stated. Look at Paragraph 1 to figure out the effect of extinction.

4   **Which of these is <u>not</u> a cause for giant pandas to be endangered?**

   F   There is not enough rain in the bamboo forests.

   G   Poachers hunt pandas for their fur.

   H   The forests are disappearing.

   J   Pandas live too far apart from each other.

1 Ⓐ Ⓑ Ⓒ Ⓓ
2 Ⓕ Ⓖ Ⓗ Ⓙ
3 Ⓐ Ⓑ Ⓒ Ⓓ
4 Ⓕ Ⓖ Ⓗ Ⓙ

STOP

Language

Skill Overview

A **complete sentence** has a subject and a verb and forms a complete thought.

A **sentence fragment** does not form a complete sentence.

Fragment	How to Correct	Corrected
Played soccer.	Add a subject.	*My friends and I played soccer.*
Our team.	Add a verb.	*Our team won the game.*

When writing a command, however, you do not need to include a subject. The subject, <u>you</u>, is understood. For example, the command *Pick up the garbage* is a complete sentence even though there is no <u>you</u>.

In a sentence that is written correctly, the subject and the verb agree. Both the subject and the verb are either singular or plural.

A **singular subject** names one person, place, thing, or idea. For example, *The girl eats an orange.* Both the subject *(girl)* and the verb *(eats)* are singular.

A **plural subject** names more than one person, place, thing, or idea. For example, *Maria, Thomas, and I do homework together. Maria, Thomas, and I* agree with the plural form of the verb *do.*

Punctuation helps readers understand sentences. **End punctuation** tells readers when to stop. End punctuation can also identify a sentence as a statement, a question, or an exclamation.

End Punctuation		
Period (.)	**Question Mark (?)**	**Exclamation Point(!)**
At the end of a statement.	At the end of a question.	To show strong feeling.
Today is Tuesday.	*What time is it?*	*I am so late!*

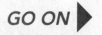
GO ON

Skill Practice

Lauren wrote this narrative. It contains mistakes. Read the narrative and answer Numbers 1 through 6.

Staying Up

(1) Most nights, had trouble falling asleep. (2) She didn't mind staying up, but she didn't like being the last one awake. (3) The dark, quiet house spooked her a little. (4) So every night at bedtime, Lauren would whisper to her parents, "Can you stay awake until I fall asleep"

(5) One day in August, Lauren's dad's aunt came to visit. (6) Lauren didn't think this visitor were much fun at all. (7) Whenever Lauren asked Aunt Blanche to play a game or go swimming, Blanche said, "Hrrmm," and goes back to her knitting.

(8) One Friday night, Lauren's parents said that they were going out and Aunt Blanche was babysitting. (9) When it was time for bed, Lauren croaked to Aunt Blanche, "Um ... Aunt Blanche ... Don't go to sleep before I do."

(10) An hour later, Lauren was still awake and sure that Aunt Blanche was sound asleep (11) Lauren tiptoed over to Aunt Blanche's room and peeked in. (12) There was Blanche, sitting bolt upright in bed, knitting, and waiting for Lauren to nod off. (13) Lauren smiled to herself, went back to her room, and fallen instantly asleep.

---

1 **Read Sentence 1.**

Most nights, had trouble falling asleep.

Which is the best way to make this a complete sentence?

A   Most nights trouble was falling asleep.

B   Most nights Lauren's trouble falling asleep.

C   Most nights Lauren had trouble falling asleep.

D   Most nights falling asleep trouble.

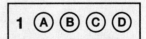

2 **Read Sentence 4.**

*So every night at bedtime, Lauren would whisper
to her parents, "Can you stay awake until I fall
asleep"*

What is the <u>best</u> punctuation mark for the end of the sentence?

F a period

G a comma

H a question mark

J an exclamation point

3 **Read Sentence 7.**

*Whenever Lauren asked Aunt Blanche to play a
game or go swimming, Blanche said, "Hrrmm,"
<u>and goes back</u> to her knitting.*

What is the correct way to write the underlined part of the sentence?

A and go back

B and goes on back

C and went back

D and had went back

4 **Read Sentence 6.**

*Lauren didn't think this visitor <u>were</u> much fun
at all.*

What is the correct way to write the underlined word in the sentence?

F was

G are

H weren't

J wasn't

2 Ⓕ Ⓖ Ⓗ Ⓙ
3 Ⓐ Ⓑ Ⓒ Ⓓ
4 Ⓕ Ⓖ Ⓗ Ⓙ

GO ON ▶

5 **Read Sentence 10.**

An hour later, Lauren was still awake and sure
that Aunt Blanche was sound asleep

What is the <u>best</u> punctuation mark for the end of the sentence?

A exclamation point

B comma

C semi colon

D period

6 **Read Sentence 13.**

Lauren smiled to herself, went back to her room,
<u>*and fallen instantly*</u> *asleep.*

Which is the correct way to write the underlined part of the sentence?

F and fell instantly

G and fell instant

H and falls instantly

J and felled instantly

5 Ⓐ Ⓑ Ⓒ Ⓓ
6 Ⓕ Ⓖ Ⓗ Ⓙ

Responding to a Prompt

Skill Overview

Sometimes you will be asked to respond to a **writing prompt**. The prompt will tell you what kind of writing to do. Before you begin to write, read the prompt twice to make sure you understand it.

Step 1: Planning Your Writing

Think about the kind of writing you will do. For example, the word <u>explain</u> is a clue that you will be writing nonfiction. The words <u>character</u> or <u>setting</u> will help you know that you will be writing a kind of narrative. As you write, keep thinking about the kind of writing the prompt is asking for.

Once you know the kind of writing to do, you need to plan and organize it. Lists, word webs, and freewrites can help you come up with ideas. Story maps and idea-support maps can help you organize what you want to say.

Step 2: Writing a First Draft

You can use the ideas in your graphic organizer or freewrite to write a first draft. For this step, you should not worry about perfect sentences. This is when you should develop your topic and connect your ideas. Consider a beginning, a middle, and an ending for fiction or an introduction, a body, and a conclusion for nonfiction. Remember to write in your own voice.

Step 3: Revising Your Writing

When you revise, you make changes to improve your first draft. You make your writing clearer and more interesting by adding or removing words or details or by changing the order of your sentences. Make sure your writing stays on topic.

Step 4: Editing Your Writing

The editing step is when you correct any spelling or grammar errors you may have made. If you have an editing checklist, now is the time to use it.

Step 5: Writing a Final Draft

The last step is writing your final draft. During this step, you rewrite your paper and put in all the changes you made during the revising and editing steps. Also, make sure your work is neat and written in a handwriting that everyone can read.

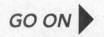

GO ON

17

Name _____ Date _____

Writing to Narrate

A writing prompt tells you what to write. One type of writing you may be asked to do is narrative. Narrative writing can be realistic fiction, fantasy, or a true story about you or someone you know.

Directions   Read the prompt.

Writing Situation: Pretend you are in your classroom when, suddenly, a group of penguins enters the room.

Directions for Writing: Before you begin writing, think about why the penguins came into the room and what happens next.

Now write a story about what happens in your classroom with the penguins.

Planning Page

Directions   Use this space to plan your writing. Write your response on your own sheet of paper.

_____

_____

_____

_____

_____

_____

Name _____ Date _____

Suffixes

Skill Overview

You might have read some unknown words in *Invasion from Mars*. Some of those words, such as <u>indescribable</u> and <u>rimless</u>, had suffixes that could help you figure out the meaning.

Figuring out the meaning of an unknown word calls for some "detective work." You can sometimes use context clues. Other clues can come from the word itself.

A **root word** is the main part of a word that gives the word its meaning. Some root words have word parts added to them. An **affix** is a word part added to a root word to change its meaning. A **suffix** is an affix added to the end of a word.

You can use the meanings of **suffixes** to figure out how they change the meanings of root words. Suffixes may sometimes change the part of speech of a word. For example, the suffixes *-ous* and *-y* change nouns into adjectives. Look at their meanings in the chart below.

Suffix	Meaning	Example
-ous	"full of"	joyous (full of joy)
-y	"in a state of"	misty

When you look at an unknown word, see if it has a suffix. Study the root word and the suffix. Think about how the suffix changes the meaning of the root word.

GO ON ▶

Skill Practice

Directions Read the article. Then answer Numbers 1 through 4.

An Enjoyable New Sport

1   Do you like to get out in the country? Do you feel comfortable on a bike? If so, when you grow up, you should try an event called cyclocross. In this demanding sport, you have to ride your bike and carry it!

2   You spend only part of the race on your bike because only half of the course is smooth. That half runs over pavement, smooth grass, and trails. The other half is harder. It goes though country fields, where bikers make their way over bumpy trails and up steep, woodsy hills. Bikers must even get over logs, sandpits, mud puddles, fences, and piles of wood. Several times during the race, riders must swiftly hop off their bikes. Then they hang their bikes over their shoulders and run as fast as their legs will carry them.

3   Determining when to ride and where to run is part of the strategy. At some points, hurdles force riders off their bikes. These hurdles are 10 to 15 inches high and are set close together. Racers must jump over the hurdles. As you can imagine, this is a perilous sport. There are dangers at every turn, so racers cannot be careless.

TIP

When you come across an unknown word, look for a familiar root word or suffix.

TIP

Separate a word into its root word and suffix by circling the suffix and underlining the root word. Then look at each part separately to figure out its meaning.

4   Races are fast and furious and last less than an hour from start to finish. A rider might be able to practice on an actual course to prepare for a race. Sometimes a rider can revisit a course to train.

5   Cyclocross bikes are like racing bikes, light in weight and with turned-down handlebars. Tires are narrow, but they have deep ruts in them that help the bikes get through dirt and mud.

6   Cyclocross began in Europe about fifteen years ago. The idea was to keep cyclists fit and healthy during the winter, as well as to help riders develop their skills and strength.

7   So, if you work out an hour a day, three or four days a week, you will probably be strong enough to compete. Don't get the wrong idea, though. The training is difficult, and the races themselves certainly can be dangerous. If you are strong, daring, and looking for adventure, then cyclocross might be just the thing for you.

> **TIP**
>
> You can put the meanings of a root word and suffix together to identify an unknown word.

1 **Read the sentence from Paragraph 2.**

It goes though country fields, where bikers make their way over <u>bumpy</u> trails and up steep, woodsy hills.

What is the meaning of the word <u>bumpy</u>?

A   without bumps

B   not able to have bumps

C   in a state of having bumps

D   making large bumps on a soft surface

> **TIP**
>
> The word bumpy has the root word "bump" and the suffix -y. Think about how the suffix changes the meaning of the root word.

1 (A) (B) (C) (D)

GO ON ▶

Name _____ Date _____

2 **Read the sentence from Paragraph 3.**

As you can imagine, this is a perilous sport.

What is the meaning of the word perilous?

F full of peril

G able to be in peril

H the action of peril

J one who is not in peril

> **TIP**
>
> Reminder: Peril means danger.

3 **Read the sentence from Paragraph 4.**

Races are fast and furious and last less than an hour from start to finish.

What is the meaning of the word furious?

A without fury

B filled with fury

C an act of extreme fury

D able to build fires quickly

> **TIP**
>
> Remember to underline the root word and circle its suffix. What do the two parts mean? Put the two parts together to figure out the word's meaning.

4 **Read the sentence from Paragraph 6.**

The idea was to keep cyclists fit and healthy during the winter, as well as to help riders develop their skills and strength.

What is the meaning of the word healthy?

F without health

G not completely safe

H in a state of good health

J to do something against good health

2 Ⓕ Ⓖ Ⓗ Ⓙ
3 Ⓐ Ⓑ Ⓒ Ⓓ
4 Ⓕ Ⓖ Ⓗ Ⓙ

STOP

Responding to a Prompt

Skill Overview

Sometimes you will be asked to respond to a **writing prompt**. The prompt will tell you what kind of writing to do. Before you begin to write, read the prompt twice to make sure you understand it.

Step 1: Planning Your Writing

Think about the kind of writing you will do. For example, the word <u>explain</u> is a clue that you will be writing nonfiction. The words <u>character</u> or <u>setting</u> will help you know that you will be writing a kind of narrative. As you write, keep thinking about the kind of writing the prompt is asking for.

Once you know the kind of writing to do, you need to plan and organize it. Lists, word webs, and freewrites can help you come up with ideas. Story maps and idea-support maps can help you organize what you want to say.

Step 2: Writing a First Draft

You can use the ideas in your graphic organizer or freewrite to write a first draft. For this step, you should not worry about perfect sentences. This is when you should develop your topic and connect your ideas. Consider a beginning, a middle, and an ending for fiction or an introduction, a body, and a conclusion for nonfiction. Remember to write in your own voice.

Step 3: Revising Your Writing

When you revise, you make changes to improve your first draft. You make your writing clearer and more interesting by adding or removing words or details or by changing the order of your sentences. Make sure your writing stays on topic.

Step 4: Editing Your Writing

The editing step is when you correct any spelling or grammar errors you may have made. If you have an editing checklist, now is the time to use it.

Step 5: Writing a Final Draft

The last step is writing your final draft. During this step, you rewrite your paper and put in all the changes you made during the revising and editing steps. Also, make sure your work is neat and written in a handwriting that everyone can read.

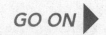
GO ON

Writing to Inform

A writing prompt tells you what to write. One type of writing you may be asked to do is informational. It might be instructions, a description, a report, or an explanation.

Directions   Read the prompt.

Writing Situation: Pretend you have to teach a friend how to make or do something.

Directions for Writing: Before you begin writing, think about something you would like to teach a friend to do or make.

Now write an essay to tell how to do or make it.

Planning Page

Directions   Use this space to plan your writing. Write your response on your own sheet of paper.

_____

_____

_____

_____

_____

_____

_____

Figurative Language

Skill Overview

In *Me and Uncle Romie,* the author uses phrases like "Uncle Romie's voice was like thunder" and "on top of the world." These phrases are examples of figurative language.

You will sometimes read phrases that you do not understand. You might know the meaning of each word, but the words together can be confusing. For example, you may know the words *get, cold,* and *feet,* but not the meaning of *get cold feet.*

> Before I go on stage, I <u>get cold feet</u>.

The phrase *get cold feet* is an example of figurative language. **Figurative language** uses vivid images or comparisons to create pictures in the reader's mind. Figurative language does not mean exactly what it says, so you have to figure it out. You can use nearby words as clues.

Idioms, similes, and metaphors are types of figurative language. An **idiom** is a familiar, commonly-used expression that does not have a word-for-word translation. You can use context clues to figure out the meaning.

> I love hiking and would do it <u>at the drop of a hat</u>.

Context clues show that the speaker loves to hike. The expression *at the drop of a hat* means "right away" or "at any time."

A **simile** uses the words <u>like</u> or <u>as</u> to compare ideas or things.

> Doug runs <u>as</u> fast <u>as</u> a cheetah.

A **metaphor** compares two things without using <u>like</u> or <u>as</u>.

> Life is a dream.

When you come across figurative language you do not understand, remember to use context clues to determine the meaning.

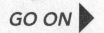

GO ON

Name _____ Date _____

Skill Practice

Directions Read the story. Then answer Numbers 1 through 6.

The After-School Club

1 Billy belonged to an after-school club. The purpose was to have fun while learning something new. Each week, a different member planned and ran the meeting. This week, it was Billy's turn. He was in the doghouse with the other members. The last time it was his turn, he cancelled the meeting, so he really needed to do something out of the ordinary to make it up to the group.

2 This week, he had everyone take a seat around the club's table. On the table was a large silk cloth covering objects. Billy snapped the cloth up from the table, like a magician performing a trick. All of the members looked with curiosity at the variety of items in front of them.

3 "You have only two minutes to memorize as many items as you can," Billy said. "It's a race against the clock." He produced a stopwatch from his pocket and, after yelling, "Go!" pushed the button. As the clock ticked, everyone concentrated on the objects. Their eyes were saucers, wide and unblinking. Then Billy announced that time was up and covered up the objects. He asked how many items each club member remembered.

4 "I remember scissors, a spoon, a sugar cube, and a strainer!" said Jan excitedly. "I memorized things that began with the same letter."

5 "I remember an apple, a cup, a glove, a rope, and a watch," Marco said. "I put things in alphabetical order."

6 "I remember the scissors and the knife, the thread and the rope, and the cup and the glass," said Ileana. "I tried to think of things that were similar in some way."

7 "I remember the glove, the rope, the apple, the strainer, and the scissors," said Rick, explaining that he used the first letters of some of the objects to make a word—GRASS.

TIP
If something you read sounds odd at first, it might be figurative language. Stop and try to figure out the meaning from nearby word clues.

TIP
Sometimes you can figure out an expression by picturing what it says. Reread how Billy took the cloth off the objects, "like a magician performing a trick." Imagine what it looks like. That picture can help you figure out what the expression means.

TIP
Word clues are usually found near the unknown expression. They can come before or after it, however.

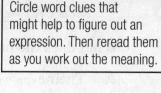
8   "Each of you had a different trick that helped you remember what you saw," said Billy. "I'll bet there are even more memory tricks that we should find out about!"

9   The members all agreed that Billy's club meeting was one of the best they'd ever had. They all had fun, and the meeting flew by in a flash. Billy was as proud as a peacock.

---

1   **Read the sentence from Paragraph 1.**

He was in the doghouse with the other members.

What is the meaning of the idiom in the doghouse?

A   in trouble

B   ready to go

C   not prepared

D   popular with others

2   **Read the sentence from Paragraph 2.**

Billy snapped the cloth up from the table, like a magician performing a trick.

Which choice best describes this expression?

F   a simile that describes how Billy acts

G   an idiom that describes how Billy feels

H   a metaphor that describes how Billy acts

J   a simile that describes what a magic trick looks like

1 Ⓐ Ⓑ Ⓒ Ⓓ
2 Ⓕ Ⓖ Ⓗ Ⓙ

GO ON ▶

3 **Read the sentence from Paragraph 3.**

Their eyes were saucers, wide and unblinking.

What does the metaphor their eyes were saucers mean?

A Their eyes were hard and cold.

B Their eyes were almost closed shut.

C Their eyes were opened wide and round.

D Their eyes showed that they were very hungry.

> **TIP**
> Think about what saucers would look like in place of someone's eyes to figure out the meaning of this metaphor.

4 **Read the sentence from Paragraph 3.**

"It's a race against the clock."

What does it mean to race against the clock?

F The clocks are running fast.

G There can be only one winner.

H It is time to stop doing the activity.

J There is little time to finish the task.

5 **Read the sentence from Paragraph 9.**

They all had fun, and the meeting flew by in a flash.

What does the expression in a flash mean?

A completely

B quickly

C quietly

D smoothly

> **TIP**
> The club members are having fun. How does time go by for you when you are having fun?

6 **Read the sentence from Paragraph 9.**

Billy was as proud as a peacock.

What does this simile mean?

F Billy acted like a bird.

G Billy looked like a peacock.

H Billy thought peacocks were fancy.

J Billy felt like a pleased, strutting peacock.

3 Ⓐ Ⓑ Ⓒ Ⓓ
4 Ⓕ Ⓖ Ⓗ Ⓙ
5 Ⓐ Ⓑ Ⓒ Ⓓ
6 Ⓕ Ⓖ Ⓗ Ⓙ

STOP

Writing and Research

Skill Overview

When you sit down to write, one of the first things you should think about is your **purpose**, or your reason for writing. You might write to inform, or give facts and details; to entertain, or tell a story; or to respond, or give opinions. The writing you do will depend on your purpose.

One way to determine your purpose for writing is to think about your **audience**, or for whom you are writing. Ask yourself if you're writing for a teacher or other adult, a friend, or a classmate. The words you choose and the language you use will be a little different for each different audience. For example, you would use less formal language for your friends and more formal language for a teacher. Say you wanted to write about a littering problem at your school. How would your letter be different if you were writing to your friends or writing to the principal?

Audience	Language
friends	Hey! There is too much trash on the school grounds. It feels like we live in a garbage dump sometimes.
principal	The littering problem in our school needs to be addressed. We should have signs and programs that remind students not to litter.

Keep your audience and purpose in mind as you write. Also keep in mind that the **details** in a paragraph should support your main idea or **topic sentence**. When you revise, look out for information that doesn't belong. Your sentences should also follow a logical order, such as retelling events in the order they happened or listing reasons in order from least to most important.

GO ON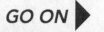

Skill Practice

Directions   Walker wrote this report about his art class. It contains mistakes. Read the report and answer Numbers 1 through 6.

1   We had an unusual art class today. Art is my favorite class of the day. We usually use paper as the "surface" and apply paint, ink, or crayons to it. Today, we used the paper as the "medium" and folded it into sculptures.

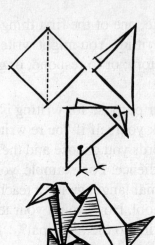

2   Our teacher introduced a guest named Mr. Tanaka. Mr. Tanaka said that he would teach us *origami*, the traditional Japanese art of paper folding. He explained that the word comes from *oru* meaning "folding" and *kami* meaning "paper."

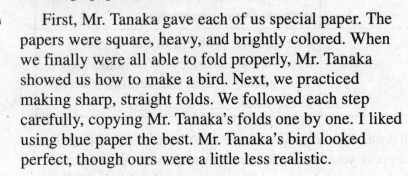

3   First, Mr. Tanaka gave each of us special paper. The papers were square, heavy, and brightly colored. When we finally were all able to fold properly, Mr. Tanaka showed us how to make a bird. Next, we practiced making sharp, straight folds. We followed each step carefully, copying Mr. Tanaka's folds one by one. I liked using blue paper the best. Mr. Tanaka's bird looked perfect, though ours were a little less realistic.

4   We all tried again. I eventually made a bird that looked pretty good. Mr. Tanaka then folded paper into amazing dinosaurs, ladybugs, and designs that moved. I plan to practice origami a lot so I can make a dinosaur someday, too!

1 For which audience is this report <u>most likely</u> written?

   A origami experts

   B people interested in art classes

   C people interested in birds

   D accomplished artists

> **TIP**
> Think about whom Walker could be writing for. The audience for a piece is often related to its purpose.

2 Which sentence would be <u>best</u> to add to the beginning of Paragraph 3 as the topic sentence?

   F Mr. Tanaka walked us through the steps.

   G Mr. Tanaka likes birds.

   H Making origami is really boring.

   J He can make many kinds of animals.

3 Which detail <u>best</u> supports the ideas in Paragraph 4?

   A Everyone got better with practice.

   B Origami is a very old art form.

   C Mr. Tanaka likes to make origami.

   D I like birds.

> **TIP**
> The first sentence of a paragraph is usually the topic sentence. Remember that all detail sentences in a paragraph must support the topic sentence.

4 Which sentence from Paragraph 1 should be deleted?

   F We had an unusual art class today.

   G Art is my favorite class of the day.

   H We usually use paper as the "surface" and apply paint, ink, or crayons to it.

   J Today, we used the paper as the "medium" and folded it into sculptures.

1 Ⓐ Ⓑ Ⓒ Ⓓ
2 Ⓕ Ⓖ Ⓗ Ⓙ
3 Ⓐ Ⓑ Ⓒ Ⓓ
4 Ⓕ Ⓖ Ⓗ Ⓙ

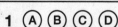
GO ON ▶

5 **Read these sentences from Paragraph 3.**

1. First, Mr. Tanaka gave each of us special paper.
2. The papers were square, heavy, and brightly colored.
3. When we finally were all able to fold properly, Mr. Tanaka showed us how to make a bird.
4. Next, we practiced making sharp, straight folds.

What is the <u>best</u> order for these sentences?

A 1, 2, 3, 4

B 2, 3, 4, 1

C 1, 2, 4, 3

D 4, 3, 2, 1

6 **Which sentence does <u>not</u> belong in Paragraph 3?**

F Next, we practiced making sharp, straight folds.

G We followed each step carefully, copying Mr. Tanaka's folds one by one.

H I liked using blue paper the best.

J Mr. Tanaka's bird looked perfect, though ours were a little less realistic.

5 (A) (B) (C) (D)
6 (F) (G) (H) (J)

STOP

Poetry

Skill Overview

Poems often use the way words sound to show meaning. Some poems have a rhythm that you can count out in beats. Some poems use rhyming words. Some poems use onomatopoeia to help you "hear" the sounds the writer is describing. The chart below shows some of the tools writers use in their poems.

rhyme	lines that end the same way *Broken gravel covers the street.* *It really is rough on your feet!*
alliteration	words that start with the same sound *Sarah sells socks on State Street.* *Tammy tells tales to Tanya.*
simile	comparisons using <u>like</u> or <u>as</u> *The leather felt as smooth as butter.* *Dad was angry and roared like a lion.*
metaphor	comparisons *Julie's home run was a real rocket.*
antonyms	opposites *The sand was not rough; it was soft and smooth fabric across the shore.*
onomatopoeia	words that say their own sound *buzz, beep*
repetition	lines, phrases, or ideas that are repeated in a poem

GO ON ▶

Name _____ Date _____

Skill Practice

Directions   Read the poem. Then answer Numbers 1 through 4.

Waiting for Dinner

1   A tiger and bear
Were lying in a cave.
The tiger began growling,
And the bear said, "You behave."

5   The tiger whined, "I'm hungry,
I've had nothing to eat for hours,"
The bear said, "Stop your grumbling
And take time to smell the flowers."

The angry tiger bellowed,
10   "Flowers won't fill my tummy!"
And the bear replied calmly,
"But their scent is just like honey."

The tiger leaped out of the cave,
In search of something tasty.
15   He ran right into a super swarm
Of angry honeybees.

The bear smelled all the flowers
That surrounded his hollow home
Then quietly followed the buzzing bees
20   Back to their honeycomb.

As he licked the dripping honey
Off his paws and ate for hours
The bear said, "I told the tiger
To take time to smell the flowers."

34

Name _____ Date _____

1 How can you tell that "Waiting for Dinner" is a poem? Give <u>two</u> details to support your answer.

_____

_____

_____

_____

2 Which line or lines from the poem include examples of alliteration? How do you know?

_____

_____

_____

_____

GO ON ▶

3 Find <u>two</u> pairs of rhyming words in the poem. How do you know they rhyme?

_____

_____

_____

_____

4 What is an example of repetition in the poem? How is it used?

_____

_____

_____

_____

36

Language

Skill Overview

A noun names a person, place, or thing. A proper noun names a specific person, place, thing, or idea. When writing, use a capital letter to signal that a word is a proper noun.

Proper Noun Rule	
People or Groups	Richard James, Girl Scouts, Americans
Personal Titles	Aunt Debbie, Dr. Carter, Mr. Edwards
Places	Grand Canyon, Warwick Street

Apostrophes can be used to identify possessive nouns, or ownership. For example, *The teacher used Mary's pen to grade the students' papers.*

A pronoun can take the place of a noun in a sentence.

Pronoun Rule	Example
A pronoun must agree with the noun it replaces.	Incorrect: *The dog found the bone and ate <u>them</u>.* Correct: *The dog found the bone and ate <u>it</u>.*
Use the correct case, or form, of a pronoun.	Incorrect: *The students opened they books.* Correct: *The students opened <u>their</u> books.*

In a sentence that is written correctly, the subject and the verb agree. Both the subject and the verb are either singular or plural.

Avoid using double negatives when you write. A **double negative** happens when two negative words are used in one sentence. Negative words include *no, not, never, none, nothing,* and *nobody.* Incorrect: *They do not like no loud noises.* Correct: *They do not like loud noises.*

Be careful to spell words correctly and remember to use spelling patterns you know.

GO ON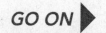

Skill Practice

Directions   Tami wrote this narrative. It contains mistakes. Read the narrative and answer Numbers 1 through 6.

Riding a Horse

(1) My uncle have a ranch in Nashville, Tennessee. (2) When I went to visit him, I got to rid his horse. (3) At first, I did not want to ride no horse. (4) I had never been close to a horse before. (5) My uncle put him arm on my shoulder to comfort me. (6) "Put your foot in the horse's stirrup and grab the saddle as high as you can reach," said Uncle Frank. (7) He told me to pull myself up and swing my other leg over the horse. (8) When I was sitting on the saddle, Uncle Frank handed me the rains. (9) I held on while my uncle led the horse a few steps. (10) He told me, "Pull the left rein to go left, and pull the right rein to go right." (11) When I wanted to stop, I pull both reins and said, "Whoa!" (12) I hope I can ride Uncle Franks' horse again soon.

1   **Read Sentence 1.**

My uncle have a ranch in Nashville, Tennessee.

Which is the correct way to write the underlined part of the sentence?

A   My uncle is having

B   My uncle has

C   My uncle had

D   My uncle having

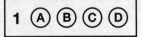

2 **Read Sentence 2.**

When I went to visit him, I got to rid his horse.

Which is the correct way to write the underlined word?

F read

G rode

H ride

J correct as is

3 **Read Sentence 3.**

At first, I did not want to ride no horse.

What is the correct way to write the sentence?

A At first, I did not want to ride a horse.

B At first, I want to ride no horse.

C At first, I did not ride no horse.

D At first, I never wanted to ride any horse.

4 **Read Sentence 5.**

My uncle put him arm on my shoulder to comfort me.

Which is the correct way to write the underlined part of the sentence?

F put he's arm

G put his arm

H put my arm

J correct as is

2 Ⓕ Ⓖ Ⓗ Ⓙ

3 Ⓐ Ⓑ Ⓒ Ⓓ

4 Ⓕ Ⓖ Ⓗ Ⓙ

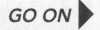 **GO ON**

39

Name _____ Date _____

5 **Read Sentence 8.**

When I was sitting on the saddle, Uncle Frank handed me the <u>rains</u>.

Which is the correct way to write the underlined word?

A reigns

B raynes

C reins

D correct as is

6 **Read Sentence 11.**

When I wanted to stop, I <u>pull</u> *both reins and said, "Whoa!"*

Which is the correct way to write the underlined word?

F pulled

G pulls

H pulling

J have pulled

5 Ⓐ Ⓑ Ⓒ Ⓓ
6 Ⓕ Ⓖ Ⓗ Ⓙ

STOP

Synonyms and Antonyms

Skill Overview

The selection *The Earth Dragon Awakes* includes word pairs such as <u>shout</u> and <u>holler</u>, in which the words have roughly the same meaning. It also includes word pairs such as <u>creep</u> and <u>bolt</u>, in which the words have opposite meanings.

Words that have the same or similar meanings are called **synonyms**. In the sentence below, the words <u>stop</u> and <u>cease</u> are synonyms.

> When the coach tells us to <u>stop</u>, we <u>cease</u> running right away.

Words that have opposite meanings are known as **antonyms**. In the sentence below, the words <u>entertaining</u> and <u>dull</u> are antonyms.

> I thought the movie was <u>entertaining</u>, but my sister thought it was very <u>dull</u>.

Synonyms and antonyms can help you figure out unknown words. Look for words such as <u>but</u>. In the sentence about the movie, the word <u>but</u> tells you that the speaker and the sister hold very different opinions about the movie. If you knew what <u>dull</u> meant, you could use that information to find out the meaning of <u>entertaining</u>: <u>entertaining</u> would mean more or less the opposite of <u>dull</u>.

Synonyms and antonyms can also help you solve analogies. An **analogy** compares two pairs of words that have the same relationship.

> wet : dry :: hot : cold

You can read this as "wet is related to dry in the same way that hot is related to cold." Check that this is true: <u>wet</u> and <u>dry</u> are antonyms, and <u>hot</u> and <u>cold</u> are antonyms, too. The relationship connects the words in each pair in the same way.

In an analogy problem, the last word is often missing. Your job is to find it by thinking about the relationship between the first pair of words, and then by applying that relationship to the second pair of words. Here is an example:

> smart : intelligent :: difficult : _____

<u>Smart</u> and <u>intelligent</u> are synonyms. The words in the other pair must be synonyms too. So, the missing word must mean roughly the same as <u>difficult</u> such as <u>hard</u>, <u>tough</u>, or <u>rugged</u>.

GO ON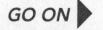

Skill Practice

Directions   Read the article. Then answer Numbers 1 through 4.

John Ringling

1   John Ringling was a businessman, a circus owner, an art collector, and more. He was born on May 31, 1866, in Iowa. As a young man, Ringling decided to start a circus with his brothers. Their plan was to travel from one town to another, performing as they went. Although John Ringling appeared in the show at first, he soon became bored with performing and realized he was more interested in helping to run the business. Soon he took on the job of deciding what towns the circus would visit and in what order. Ringling traveled to those towns ahead of the circus to tell people about it and make them eager to see the show in person.

2   John Ringling also made some important changes in the way the brothers' circus operated. In 1890, for instance, he convinced his brothers that the circus should travel by train. Before that, every member of the circus—and every piece of equipment as well— traveled in wagons pulled by horses. Soon the Ringling Brothers Circus had its own train, which included almost 100 cars. It took that many to transport all the people, animals, and gear the circus required. Compared to the slow and exhausting wagon travel that the Ringlings had used earlier, train travel was swift and easy.

3   In 1907, Ringling and his brothers purchased the Barnum and Bailey Circus. Though the Barnum and Bailey Circus had been both large and very well-known, it was beginning to lose money, and its owners were happy to sell out to the Ringlings. The expansion made the Ringling Brothers' circus one of the largest in the country. Once, John Ringling and his brothers had been obscure circus performers. Now, the Ringling Brothers were famous everywhere they went.

TIP

Remember that synonyms mean more or less the same thing. What would be a synonym for business in this paragraph?

TIP

Clue words and phrases like although, but, and compared to often signal that a pair of words in a paragraph are antonyms.

TIP

Remember that antonyms have opposite meanings. Look for words that are opposites. Antonyms often tell how things are different.

Name _____ Date _____

4   Profits from the circus soon made John Ringling quite wealthy. He began investing his money in other businesses, including oil companies and railroads. Ringling became especially interested in buying land in towns and cities along the Gulf Coast. He built houses and hotels on his new land, hoping to turn municipalities into vacation destinations.

5   Besides circuses and real estate, Ringling was also deeply interested in art. He spent much of his wealth on famous paintings and sculptures. Toward the end of the 1920s, Ringling used his fortune to build a museum near his home so he could display his artworks. The museum was built in part with the assistance of elephants from Ringling's own circus; they provided help in putting the stones where they belonged. Though Ringling died in 1936 at the age of 70, the museum remains open to visitors.

TIP

Notice that <u>towns</u> and <u>cities</u> and <u>municipalities</u> are used in similar ways in this paragraph. You can use <u>towns</u> and <u>cities</u> and what you know about synonyms to figure out what <u>municipalities</u> means.

1   **Which word from the article <u>best</u> completes this analogy?**

worried : anxious :: enthusiastic : _____

   A   bored

   B   eager

   C   travel

   D   visit

TIP

How are the first two words related to each other? If they are synonyms, then the words in the second pair must be synonyms, too. If they are antonyms, the words in the second pair must be antonyms as well.

1 Ⓐ Ⓑ Ⓒ Ⓓ   *GO ON* ▶

2 **Read the sentence from Paragraph 2.**

Compared to the slow and exhausting wagon travel that the Ringlings had used earlier, train travel was swift and easy.

Which word has the opposite meaning of the word slow?

F easy

G exhausting

H sluggish

J swift

TIP

What phrase begins the sentence that slow appears in? What does that phrase often tell you about how word pairs are related?

3 **Which words from the article are opposite in meaning?**

A money, profits

B obscure, famous

C purchased, interested

D expansion, largest

4 **Read the sentence from Paragraph 5.**

He spent much of his wealth on famous paintings and sculptures.

Which word has almost the same meaning as the word wealth?

F assistance

G famous

H fortune

J heavy

2 (F) (G) (H) (J)
3 (A) (B) (C) (D)
4 (F) (G) (H) (J)

STOP ⬛

Responding to a Prompt

Skill Overview

Sometimes you will be asked to respond to a **writing prompt**. The prompt will tell you what kind of writing to do. Before you begin to write, read the prompt twice to make sure you understand it.

Step 1: Planning Your Writing

Think about the kind of writing you will do. For example, the word <u>explain</u> is a clue that you will be writing nonfiction. The words <u>character</u> or <u>setting</u> will help you know that you will be writing a kind of narrative. As you write, keep thinking about the kind of writing the prompt is asking for.

Once you know the kind of writing to do, you need to plan and organize it. Lists, word webs, and freewrites can help you come up with ideas. Story maps and idea-support maps can help you organize what you want to say.

Step 2: Writing a First Draft

You can use the ideas in your graphic organizer or freewrite to write a first draft. For this step, you should not worry about perfect sentences. This is when you should develop your topic and connect your ideas. Consider a beginning, a middle, and an ending for fiction or an introduction, a body, and a conclusion for nonfiction. Remember to write in your own voice.

Step 3: Revising Your Writing

When you revise, you make changes to improve your first draft. You make your writing clearer and more interesting by adding or removing words or details or by changing the order of your sentences. Make sure your writing stays on topic.

Step 4: Editing Your Writing

The editing step is when you correct any spelling or grammar errors you may have made. If you have an editing checklist, now is the time to use it.

Step 5: Writing a Final Draft

The last step is writing your final draft. During this step, you rewrite your paper and put in all the changes you made during the revising and editing steps. Also, make sure your work is neat and written in a handwriting that everyone can read.

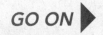

GO ON ▶

Name _____ Date _____

Writing Opinions

A writing prompt tells you what to write. One type of opinion writing you may be asked to do is a letter that persuades someone to do something or to think a certain way.

Directions Read the prompt.

Writing Situation: Imagine you can change something in your school.

Writing Directions: Before you begin writing, think about what you would like to change.

Now write a letter to your teacher telling why it should change.

Planning Page

Directions Use this space to plan your writing. Write your response on your own sheet of paper.

_____

_____

_____

_____

_____

_____

Name _____ Date _____

Text and Graphic Features

Skill Overview

The Life and Times of the Ant includes text and graphic features. The text features include headings and captions. Some of the graphic features are a timeline, a chart, and illustrations.

Text features are special types of text that help the reader find information. Headings, for example, tell what each section of a text is about.

Graphic features show information in a visual way. They include outlines, timelines, graphic organizers, charts, diagrams, maps, and illustrations.

An outline organizes the main points of a text with a title, headings, and subheadings. For example:

Benefits of a Vegetable Garden

I. Exercise

II. Food
   A. cheaper
   B. healthier
      1. more vitamins
      2. fresher

III. Environment
   A. organic
   B. local
   C. less waste

A timeline organizes events in the order they happened. For example:

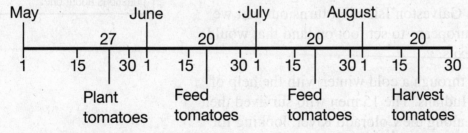

A graphic organizer shows how facts or ideas relate to each other. Examples include T-charts, story maps, and Venn diagrams.

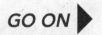

Directions Read the story. Then answer Numbers 1 through 4.

My Adventures as an Explorer

1 My name is Alvar Nuñez Cabeza de Vaca. I was born in Spain in 1490. My parents were Spanish nobles. The family name *Cabeza de Vaca* means "head of a cow."

Disaster in Florida

2 On June 17, 1527, I became an explorer, joining captain Panfilo de Narváez and a crew of 300 men sailing west. First, we went to Hispaniola, and then we sailed to Cuba, where we had some excitement—a hurricane. Storms blew our ships to a place now called "Florida." On April 12, 1528, we landed near Tampa Bay and claimed it for Spain.

3 We docked the boat and explored the land, but things quickly started going wrong. There were more hurricanes, and we fought with the natives. Food and water were scarce. Our pilot, who had stayed behind with the ship, got scared and sailed off to Mexico without us. When we returned to the ship, it was gone!

Shipwrecked

4 We wanted to get to Mexico to find the Spanish settlements, so we built five rough boats and headed off. We hit more bad weather, lost three of the boats and many of the men, and were running out of supplies. On November 6, 1528, our two remaining boats shipwrecked on Galveston Island. It turns out that we were the first Europeans to set foot on land that would later become Texas.

5 We suffered through a cold winter with the help of the Karankawa Indians. The 15 men who survived then started walking along the Colorado River, looking for food and trading with natives. For several years, we struggled for survival. By 1533, another eleven men had died.

TIP

Before reading, preview the headings to find out what each section of the story is about.

TIP

Note the dates throughout the story. They can help you create a timeline or answer questions about one.

Interesting Adventures

6   There were, however, some interesting adventures, too. For example, we were the first Europeans to see the amazing American buffalo. Some natives thought I was a medicine man, so I performed the first known surgical operation in Texas. Using a flint knife, I removed an arrowhead from a Karankawa Indian.

7   We kept walking and walking. Our trek included a walk to Mexico City, where we met the famous *conquistador* Hernán Cortés, who had conquered much of Mexico. In April 1537, I returned to Spain.

My Return to Spain

8   Back in Spain, I wrote about my adventures and about the mistreatment of natives by the Spanish conquerors. My ideas were published as *La Relacion* ("The Journal") in 1542. In 1541, I was appointed as a governor in South America. My lenient laws, however, were unpopular in Spain. So, I was recalled by the King, convicted, and then pardoned. I lived the rest of my life as a judge in Seville, Spain. I died there in 1557.

1   **Look at the timeline.**

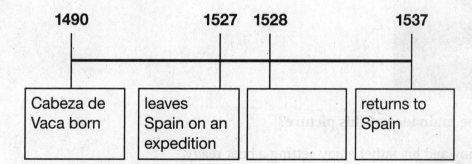

1490   1527   1528   1537

| Cabeza de Vaca born | leaves Spain on an expedition | | returns to Spain |

Which event belongs in the empty box?

A   explores Florida and Texas

B   publishes *La Relacion*

C   becomes a governor

D   moves to Seville

TIP

Skim the story, looking for events that happened in the year 1528.

1 Ⓐ Ⓑ Ⓒ Ⓓ

GO ON ▶

2 **Which section of the story gives details about Cabeza's landing in Tampa Bay?**

F Interesting Adventures

G My Return to Spain

H Disaster in Florida

J Shipwrecked

3 **Which event did <u>not</u> happen in Texas?**

A Cabeza met Cortés.

B Cabeza saw buffalo.

C Cabeza performed an operation.

D Cabeza shipwrecked on Galveston Island.

4 **Look at the picture below.**

What is the main idea of this picture?

F The boy and his father enjoy getting a boat ready.

G The people in the photo do not like boating.

H The boy is great at sailing.

J A terrible storm is coming.

2 Ⓕ Ⓖ Ⓗ Ⓙ

3 Ⓐ Ⓑ Ⓒ Ⓓ

4 Ⓕ Ⓖ Ⓗ Ⓙ

STOP

Name _____ Date _____

Main Idea and Details

Skill Overview

Ecology for Kids is mostly about the delicate balance between the environment and the organisms that live there. That message is the main idea of the passage.

Every article you read has a main idea. The **main idea** tells what the passage is mostly about.

You can look for main ideas in paragraphs, too. Each paragraph in a nonfiction passage has a main idea. The main idea of each paragraph helps tell about the main idea of the whole passage.

Sometimes it is easy to find a main idea, because the main idea is clearly stated. Other times, you need to work harder to find out what a passage or paragraph is mostly about. Supporting **details** are clues that tell about the main idea.

Details can:

- answer questions such as <u>who</u>, <u>what</u>, <u>where</u>, <u>when</u>, <u>why</u>, and <u>how</u>
- explain a main idea
- give facts, reasons, or examples that support a main idea

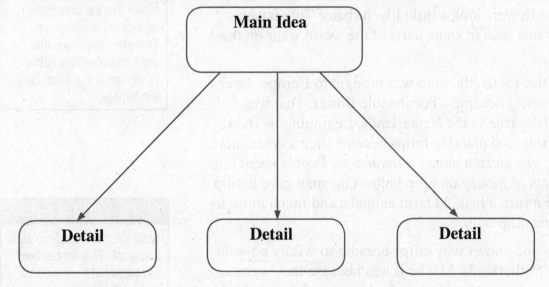

Here is an example:

Main Idea: Tennessee is important to the history of music.

- Bristol is the birthplace of country music, where the first recordings were made.
- Nashville, known as "Music City, USA," is home of the historic Grand Old Opry and the Country Music Hall of Fame.
- Memphis is the birthplace of the blues and was the center of blues music for most of the twentieth century.

GO ON ▶

Name _____ Date _____

Skill Practice

Directions Read the article. Then answer Numbers 1 through 3.

In a Tizzy for Tulips

> **TIP**
> The title often gives a hint to what the article is mostly about.

1   Can you imagine a flower that costs as much as a house? In the 1600s, someone paid that much for a red and white tulip called the *Semper Augustus*. It was the most expensive tulip in history.

2   Tulips first came from Turkey. The word *tulip* comes from a Turkish word that means "turban." The bell-shaped flowers look a little like turbans. Turbans are wraps that men in some parts of the world wear on their heads.

> **TIP**
> Notice that the word <u>turban</u> repeats in the paragraph. That gives you a clue that the most important idea in this paragraph is that tulips look like turbans.

3   In the 1500s, the tulip was brought to Europe. Over the years, it became a fashionable flower. That was especially true in the Netherlands. Beginning in 1634, collecting and planting tulips became such a craze there that it was given a name: *tulipomania*. People spent huge amounts of money on tulip bulbs. One man gave a tulip dealer a suit, a bed, 24 farm animals, and much more for just one tulip bulb.

4   No one knows why tulips became so wildly popular in the Netherlands. Maybe it was because they were so different from other flowers in that part of the world. In fact, when tulip bulbs first arrived in Europe, few people knew what they were. One merchant thought they looked like onions, so he roasted them and ate them! But once Europeans realized that the bulbs produced beautiful flowers when they were planted, they were eager to get as many tulips as they could. At first they imported the plants from Turkey, but soon they began growing bulbs

> **TIP**
> Write the main idea from each paragraph. That list can help you figure out the main idea of the entire article.

in the Netherlands and selling them to customers there and in nearby countries. Tulipomania was beginning.

5   Some people in the Netherlands bought tulips simply because the flowers were pretty and they wanted to make their gardens beautiful. But other people had different reasons for buying the plants. Many wanted to impress their friends and relatives by showing them what good taste they had. And quite a few hoped to make money by buying and selling tulips. They expected that the price of tulips would rise steadily. Then they could sell the tulips again for more money than they had originally spent. For a while this was true, as prices climbed to enormous levels. But, in 1637, people began to realize that the prices were too high. They stopped overpaying for tulips. That marked the end of tulipomania.

6   Still, tulips remain extremely popular in the Netherlands. Indeed, tulip production is a major industry in the Netherlands today. About three billion bulbs are produced there every year. Almost half of the country's land is planted with tulips! Along with wooden clogs and windmills, the tulip is considered an important symbol of the Netherlands.

> **TIP**
>
> To find the main idea of a paragraph, organize the important details in a chart. Then figure out what main idea they support.

1   **What is the main idea of Paragraph 3?**

_____

_____

_____

_____

_____

GO ON ▶

Name _____ Date _____

2 Why were people willing to pay such large sums for tulips? Give <u>two</u> details from the article to support your answer.

_____

_____

_____

_____

3 Think about how the author organized the information in the article. Complete the graphic organizer with the main idea from the article.

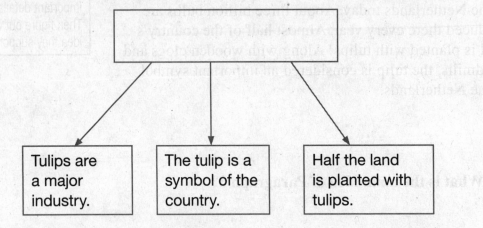

Explain why this main idea accurately completes the graphic organizer.

_____

_____

_____

_____

_____

STOP

Name _____ Date _____

Speech

Skill Overview

Giving a Speech

Giving a speech is a good way to share what you have learned, to honor a special person, or to convince people to help out with a project.

Before you write a speech, you may need to find information in books and magazines, or on the Internet, to support your ideas.

- Encyclopedias and books can give you basic facts about a topic.
- If you need the most up-to-date facts about a topic or issue, magazines and Web sites offer current information.
- Be careful to choose Web sites you can trust. For example, Web sites sponsored by the U.S. government or your state government offer reliable facts about many science and history topics.

When you give a speech, think about your purpose and audience. Speak carefully so that everyone can hear and understand your ideas. It's a good idea to include pictures, videos, or sound effects to help explain your topic and to make your speech interesting.

Listening to a Speech

Good listeners look at the speaker and pay attention. They are careful to sit quietly and not interrupt. Listen carefully for the main idea of the speech. Most speakers will explain their main point at the beginning of their speech. Once you understand the main idea, listen carefully for details that support the idea. When the speech is over, you can summarize the ideas and then ask the speaker to clarify any points you did not understand.

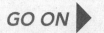

GO ON

Skill Practice

Directions Read Jacob's speech. Then answer Numbers 1 through 5.

Save the Bats!

1　　Most people are afraid of bats and think of them as creepy blood-suckers. But bats are really our friends and help us in many ways. That's why we need to save the bats and protect the places where they live.

2　　One way that bats help us is by eating mosquitoes. A single bat can eat over a thousand mosquitoes in just one hour! Bats also eat insects that damage farmers' crops. If there are enough bats around, then farmers don't need to use as many chemicals on their crops to kill insects.

3　　Some bats even pollinate the flowers of fruit trees. That means they spread the pollen from the trees' flowers, so the trees can make fruits. Bats also help spread the seeds of plants so that more of them will grow in new places.

4　　Today, some kinds of bats are in danger of dying out. That's because we are harming their habitats, the places where they live and find food. There are two kinds of bats that hibernate in Tennessee. Hibernate means that they sleep through the winter, like bears. The gray bat and the Indiana bat both hibernate in caves in Kentucky and Tennessee. Scientists are studying them so they can find ways to help save the bats.

5　　You can help keep bats alive, too. Stay out of caves where there are signs showing they are bat habitats. Don't harm bats in your neighborhood, but if you find a bat, leave it alone. Like other wild animals, bats will bite you in self-defense if you bother them, and they can spread diseases.

TIP

Look at the title and Paragraph 1 of the speech. What is the main idea Jacob wants you to know about bats?

TIP

What details in Paragraphs 2 and 3 support Jacob's main idea about bats?

1 **What is this speech mainly about?**

   A why bats are dangerous

   B how bats pollinate flowers

   C why we need to protect bats

   D where bats hibernate in winter

2 **If you were in the audience when Jacob was giving this speech, what would be the most polite thing you could do?**

   F show interest by asking questions about bats

   G help Jacob by explaining what hibernation is

   H make a list of your favorite movies about bats

   J listen carefully to Jacob and not interrupt

3 **What is the best summary of Jacob's speech?**

   A We need to beware of bats because they carry dangerous germs and are a threat to other animals.

   B We need to save bats because they eat harmful insects, pollinate flowers, and spread seeds.

   C Tennessee has more endangered bats than any other state, so it is up to us to protect them.

   D Some bats are harmful, some are harmless, and others actually help us.

1 Ⓐ Ⓑ Ⓒ Ⓓ
2 Ⓕ Ⓖ Ⓗ Ⓙ
3 Ⓐ Ⓑ Ⓒ Ⓓ

GO ON ▶

4 Which of these would be <u>best</u> for Jacob to share with the audience at the end of his speech?

    F a video showing bats pollinating flowers

    G an audio recording of the sounds bats make

    H a chart showing all Tennessee endangered animals

    J directions to the Tennessee Wildlife Resources Agency

5 Which of these would be the <u>best</u> source for learning more about endangered bats in Tennessee?

    A a nonfiction book titled *Amazing Creatures*

    B an online encyclopedia article about endangered animals

    C a magazine article called "Build Your Own Bat House"

    D a government Web site about Tennessee wildlife

4 Ⓕ Ⓖ Ⓗ Ⓙ
5 Ⓐ Ⓑ Ⓒ Ⓓ

STOP

Name _____ Date _____

Sequence of Events

Skill Overview

In *The Right Dog for the Job*, the puppy Ira goes through a series of steps to become a service dog. First, Ira lives with a foster puppy raiser and learns basic skills. Next, he goes to service-dog training. Last, he graduates and goes to live with Don.

When authors tell a story, they usually start at the beginning and follow the steps through to the end. Telling events in the order they happen is one way that authors can connect ideas. This pattern is called **chronological order**.

As you read, look for words and phrases that the author uses to organize the **sequence of events**. These clues include <u>after</u>, <u>before</u>, <u>earlier</u>, <u>finally</u>, <u>first</u>, <u>just as</u>, <u>while</u>, <u>next</u>, <u>until</u>, and <u>yesterday</u>. Dates and times, such as <u>1971</u>, <u>April 13</u>, or <u>10:30 A.M.</u>, also help put events in order.

In this example, the story events are told in chronological order. Pay attention to clue words that help you follow the order of events. Then look at how the chart below summarizes the sequence.

> The Changs had a lot to do. First, they cleaned the house. They swept, dusted, and put things away. Next they set up tables and chairs in the yard. After that, they made burgers for the cookout. Finally, everything was ready for their guests.

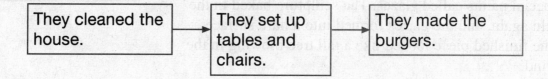

| They cleaned the house. | → | They set up tables and chairs. | → | They made the burgers. |

Name _____ Date _____

Skill Practice

Directions   Read the story. Then answer Numbers 1 through 3.

The Art Experiment

1   The yellow fliers announced that the school art contest had arrived. For years, Stan and Jill had won a prize by painting a colorful animal. This year, Jill surprised Stan by saying, "I'm tired of doing the same old thing every year. I've been learning about all different kinds of art in class. I think we should do something different."

2   Stan liked winning prizes. He had to admit, though, that it would be fun to try something new. He figured there was plenty of time to make an animal painting if the other projects didn't work out, so he agreed to Jill's idea.

3   The next weekend, their neighbor Mrs. Franco taught Stan and Jill pottery in her basement studio. First, they kneaded clay to make it soft. Next, they rolled the clay into slabs and coils. Stan and Jill made the pieces into a sculpture. Then Mrs. Franco baked the sculpture in a hot oven called a kiln. After it cooled, they painted it with special paints called glazes. The sculpture baked in the kiln again, and the glazes formed into a hard surface. The finished piece looked like a tall tree blowing in the wind.

TIP
Paragraph 3 has many time-order words to help you figure out the order of events. Look for them and read them carefully.

4   A week later, Stan and Jill tried papier-mâché. They mixed flour and hot water. While the paste cooled, they built a cardboard armature, or frame, by taping paper towel rolls and cardboard box pieces into the shape of a pig. Then they dipped strips of newspaper in the flour paste and wrapped them around the frame. When the sticky paper dried and turned hard, Stan and Jill painted the pig hot pink. It looked a little crooked, but very cheerful.

TIP
The author tells you the steps for making papier-mâché in order. Retell the steps in your own words to remember the sequence of events.

5   Finally, Stan and Jill built a model plane with popsicle sticks, macaroni, and toothpicks. They sketched a plan and then started gluing the pieces together. Once the glue dried, they painted the plane and signed their names in tiny letters, one on each wing.

TIP
How do you know that model building is the last project? What word clues help you figure it out?

Name _____ Date _____

6   With all three projects finished, Jill asked Stan what he thought. Stan reported that he had a great time with each new project. "I might never paint another animal again," he said. "But which project will we enter in the art contest?"

7   Jill laughed and shook her head. She knew that they had a tough decision to make!

TIP

The problem in this story is that Jill surprises Stan by wanting to try something new. To figure out how the problem is solved, ask yourself, "How do things turn out for the characters?"

1 **Think about how the author organized the information in the story. Complete the timeline with one detail from the story.**

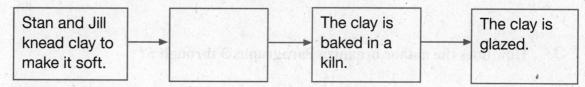

| Stan and Jill knead clay to make it soft. | → | | → | The clay is baked in a kiln. | → | The clay is glazed. |

Explain why this detail accurately completes the timeline.

_____

_____

_____

_____

_____

GO ON ▶

2 Think about how the author organized the information in the story. Complete the chart with <u>one</u> detail from the story.

1.	Jill asks Stan to try new projects.
2.	They try pottery.
3.	
4.	They build a model plane.

Explain why this detail accurately completes the chart.

_____

_____

_____

_____

3 How does the author organize Paragraphs 3 through 5?

_____

_____

_____

_____

STOP ⬛

Name _____ Date _____

Writing and Research

Skill Overview

Suppose you want to find out more about a topic for a report you are writing. You might check out a book from the library about your topic, search for information on a Web site, read a magazine or newspaper article, or look at an encyclopedia. The places you get your information are called **sources**.

You should also look for sources that have facts about your topic. For example, a story about a boy who wants to travel through time would not be a very good source for a report about the history of Tennessee. However, a book with facts about Tennessee might be a good source for your report.

Some sources are more reliable than others. How can you tell if a source is reliable? When you look at a source, ask yourself these questions:

- Is the source published by an institution, organization, or person who knows the subject well?

- If it is a Web site, can you trust it? (Sites that end in *.edu, .org* or *.gov* are usually Web sites you can trust. These were made by schools, organizations, or the government. If you're not sure about a Web site, ask your teacher or a librarian.)

- Is there background information in the author's biography or author's Web site?

- Is the source recent and up to date?

- Is the purpose or point of view of the source stated? If there is more than one side to the issue, are both sides presented?

- Is the information useful and complete?

You might also use an atlas, dictionary, or thesaurus when you revise. An atlas contains maps. A dictionary will tell you the meaning of words you don't know. A thesaurus will help you find words that mean the same thing as a different word. A thesaurus can help you find better words to use in your report.

Your title should give readers an idea of what you are writing about. It can state the topic of your writing or give clues about what the reader will see.

Also remember to use transition words in your writing to help your sentences run together smoothly and help readers understand the order of your details.

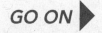
GO ON

Name _____ Date _____

Skill Practice

Directions Brian wrote a report about the General Sherman. It has mistakes. Read the report and answer Numbers 1 through 5.

1   The General Sherman is an old and famous tree. It is a kind of tree called a giant sequoia. It stands in the Giant Forest of Sequoia National Park in California. It is the largest tree on Earth.

TIP

Brian got information for his report from a few different sources. Reports contain mostly facts.

2   The General Sherman is not actually the tallest or widest tree on Earth. The tallest tree is the Hyperion tree, a coast redwood tree in northern California. There are many trees that are wider. These include giant cypress and baobab trees. All together, though, the General Sherman is the largest and oldest tree on this planet.

3   The tree was named more than 100 years ago. It got its name from an American Civil War general. The Civil War was a dark time in our nation's history. In the 1930s, scientists figured out that it is the largest tree in the world. They did this by calculating the tree's volume. _____ they compared the volume to other trees around the world. This helped them know that the General Sherman was the largest tree on Earth.

4   The General Sherman is 275 feet tall. The trunk has a diameter of about 25 feet. Scientists think the tree is 2,300–2,700 years old! You can see the General Sherman for yourself if you visit Sequoia National Park. You are bound to be impressed!

1 Read these sentences from Paragraph 3.

They did this by calculating the tree's volume. _____ they compared the volume to other trees around the world.

Which word <u>best</u> fits on the blank line?

A Next

B In fact

C At first

D In the end

2 Which title would be <u>best</u> for this report?

F The Civil War

G The World's Largest Trees

H The Largest Tree on Earth

J William Tecumseh Sherman

3 Brian wants to add more information about sequoias to his report. Which source would be <u>best</u> for him to use to begin his search?

A an article about national parks in California

B a Web site with facts about very large trees

C a friend who has been to Sequoia National Park

D a book on trees found in Tennessee

1 Ⓐ Ⓑ Ⓒ Ⓓ
2 Ⓕ Ⓖ Ⓗ Ⓙ
3 Ⓐ Ⓑ Ⓒ Ⓓ

GO ON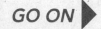

4 Look at the graphic organizer Brian made before writing his report.

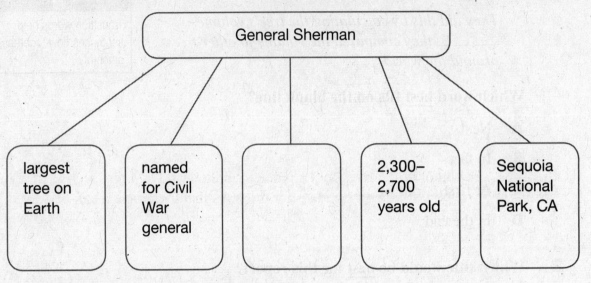

Which of these <u>best</u> fits the empty space?

F other trees are larger

G General William Tecumseh Sherman

H coast redwood trees

J scientists calculated volume to determine size

5 Brian is using a glossary to help him write his report. What information would he find in the glossary of a book on sequoias?

A a list of chapters in the book

B a list of pictures in the book

C a list of sources or articles on different topics used in writing the book

D a list of special words and definitions found in the book

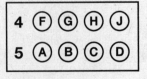

4 Ⓕ Ⓖ Ⓗ Ⓙ

5 Ⓐ Ⓑ Ⓒ Ⓓ

STOP

Name _____ Date _____

Problem and Solution

Skill Overview

The selection *Harvesting Hope* tells about the poor living conditions and unfair treatment that people faced while working on farms in California. Cesar Chavez helped solve these problems. He started the National Farm Workers Association and led a march to the California state capitol.

Authors often describe a **problem and solution** in their writings. The problem may be one that the author sees in the community, such as the need for more schools. Other times, an author will write about a problem in the world at large, such as global warming. The author will then give ideas for the ways that the problem can be solved. Plenty of facts, reasons, and examples are used to support the author's thoughts about both the problem and solutions.

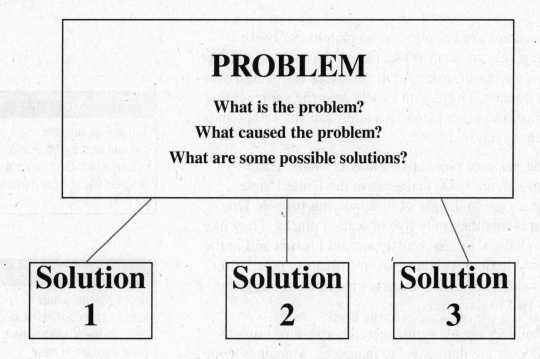

GO ON ▶

Name _____ Date _____

Skill Practice

Directions   Read the article. Then answer Numbers 1 through 3.

Protect the Manatees

1   Manatees are harmless water mammals. These gentle giants are shaped like fat torpedoes and look like walruses without tusks. Adult manatees can weigh over 2,000 pounds. They swim slowly near the shore, eating sea grass and other plants. An adult can eat 150 pounds of plants a day!

2   The manatee population today is small. There are only about 3,000 manatees in the United States. Manatees are in danger of disappearing forever. One reason is that they only live in certain places. They like warm shallow waters, mostly around Florida and in the Gulf of Mexico. Another reason is that the population grows slowly. Females usually give birth to one baby every two to five years.

3   Manatees are also endangered because of humans. Speedboats are dangerous to manatees. Manatees swim slowly and close to the surface. The blades of a fast-moving motorboat can cause serious injury or death. Humans also make the waters where manatees live less clean. Pollution threatens their survival.

4   There are ways that people can help keep manatees safe. Fast-moving boats can't see manatees until it is too late. Therefore, slow-speed zones in areas where manatees live would help protect them. Another idea is for boaters to place propeller guards on their boats.

> **TIP**
>
> Authors will state the problem near the beginning of a selection. Then they will describe one or more reasons for the problem.

> **TIP**
>
> Notice how the author uses facts and examples to describe the problem. Paying close attention to these details will give you a better understanding of the problem.

> **TIP**
>
> Carefully reading each topic sentence will tell you when the author moves from describing the problem to talking about solutions.

5   People can also protect the water where manatees live. They can limit building on nearby land and reduce chemicals that run into the water. Protecting manatees in these ways may help ensure that these interesting and gentle creatures will be around for a long time to come.

1   **Which sentence from the article <u>best</u> states the problem that manatees face?**

    A   Adult manatees can weigh over 2,000 pounds.

    B   Manatees swim slowly and close to the surface.

    C   Manatees are in danger of disappearing forever.

    D   Females usually give birth to one baby every two to five years.

2   **Which of the following is <u>not</u> a reason for the problem that manatees face?**

    F   They only eat plants.

    G   They live only in certain places.

    H   They can be injured or killed by boats.

    J   Humans pollute the waters where manatees live.

3   **According to the author, which is one solution to the manatees' problems?**

    A   Observe manatees more closely.

    B   Remove fast-moving blades from motor boats.

    C   Create ways for manatees to give birth more often.

    D   Establish slow-speed zones in areas where manatees live.

1 Ⓐ Ⓑ Ⓒ Ⓓ
2 Ⓕ Ⓖ Ⓗ Ⓙ
3 Ⓐ Ⓑ Ⓒ Ⓓ

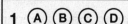

GO ON ▶

Directions   Read the letter. Then answer Numbers 4 and 5.

Pollution in Our Parks

Dear Editor,

1   Our city parks used to provide beautiful places to take a walk, enjoy nature, or have a picnic. Unfortunately, I have noticed a change in our parks over the past few years. Now the parks are littered with trash, including old cans, wrappers, and broken glass. Why has this change occurred? One reason is that there are only a few trash cans at each park, and they fill up quickly. When this happens, people leave their garbage on the ground. It also doesn't help that cuts to the city budget have reduced the number of workers who take care of the parks.

2   There are some steps that we can take to end the pollution in our parks. If the trash cans are full, visitors can put their trash in a bag and throw it away at home. People can also organize clean-up days for the parks in their neighborhoods. Last, people can vote in the next election to increase the amount of money that goes into the city's parks services department.

3   Everyone wants to enjoy our city parks. So, let's work together to make them beautiful again!

4   **What is the <u>main</u> problem that the author describes in the letter?**

   F   There are not enough trash cans in the city parks.

   G   There is no place in the city to have a picnic.

   H   The city had to make cuts to its budget.

   J   The city parks are littered with trash.

> **TIP**
>
> Think about the main point that the author is making. This will help you separate the problem from the reasons for the problem.

5   **Which solution is <u>not</u> suggested by the author?**

   A   voting to put more money into park services

   B   buying more sweepers for the parks

   C   organizing park clean-up days

   D   throwing trash away at home

> **TIP**
>
> Reread the author's solutions. Then choose the answer that does not appear in the letter.

4   Ⓕ Ⓖ Ⓗ Ⓙ
5   Ⓐ Ⓑ Ⓒ Ⓓ

Responding to a Prompt

Skill Overview

Sometimes you will be given a **writing prompt** to respond to. The prompt will explain the kind of writing you should do. Before you begin writing, read the prompt carefully to make sure you understand it.

Step 1: Planning Your Writing

Think about the kind of writing the prompt asks you to do. For example, the word describe might be a clue that you will be writing nonfiction, while the word plot might indicate that you will be writing some sort of narrative. As you write, always keep in mind the kind of writing asked for in the prompt.

For the purpose of planning and organization, you may want to use a graphic organizer, such as a story map for fiction, an idea-support map for nonfiction, or even a freewrite.

Step 2: Writing a First Draft

You can use the ideas in your graphic organizer or from your freewrite to write a first draft. Focus on developing your topic and not on perfect sentences at this point. Consider a beginning, a middle, and an ending for fiction or an introduction, a body, and a conclusion for nonfiction.

Step 3: Revising Your Writing

When you revise, you make changes to improve your draft. You can make your writing clearer and more interesting by adding or removing words or details or by changing the order of your sentences. Make sure your writing stays focused and on topic.

Step 4: Editing Your Writing

The editing stage is when you correct any spelling or grammar errors you may have. Use an editing checklist if you have one.

Step 5: Writing a Final Draft

The last step is writing your final draft. When you do your final rewrite, be sure to include all the changes you decided to make during the revising and editing stages. Also, make sure your work is neat and written in a handwriting that everyone can read.

GO ON

Name _____ Date _____

Writing to Narrate

A writing prompt tells you what to write. One type of writing you may be asked to do is narrative. Narrative writing can be realistic fiction, fantasy, or a true story about you or someone you know.

Directions   Read the prompt.

Writing Situation: Pretend you have just seen something amazing.

Directions for Writing: Before you begin writing, think about a time when you saw something amazing.

Now write a story about seeing something amazing.

Planning Page

Directions   Use this space to plan your writing. Write your response on your own sheet of paper.

_____

_____

_____

_____

_____

_____

STOP

Context Clues and Multiple-Meaning Words

Skill Overview

In *The World According to Humphrey,* you might have read words you didn't know, such as <u>bombarded</u>, <u>feats,</u> or <u>blissfully</u>. What did you do to figure out the meanings of those words?

When you read, you sometimes see unknown words or phrases. To find the meanings, you can search for **context clues**, or clues in nearby words or sentences. Context clues might:

- have the same or almost the same meaning as an unknown word

- have the opposite meaning as an unknown word

- explain, give examples of, or describe an unknown word

Read this example.

> The truck unloaded an <u>immense</u> mound of dirt in the garden. The pile was just huge!

The word <u>immense</u> means almost the same thing as <u>huge</u>.

Sometimes words used together make an expression you have never heard. Read this example.

> Celia's office was a <u>dog-eat-dog world</u>. Everyone there was very competitive.

Context clues tell you that a <u>dog-eat-dog world</u> means a place where people compete with each other and care only about their own success.

Context clues can help you figure out multiple-meaning words. A **multiple-meaning word** has more than one meaning.

> Twenty kids were <u>present</u> for the party. Everyone who came brought Jorge a nice <u>present</u>.

In the first sentence, <u>present</u> means "in attendance" or "there." In the second sentence, <u>present</u> means "gift."

GO ON ▶

Skill Practice

Directions Read the story. Then answer Numbers 1 through 4.

Queen of the House

1   Violet the cat was the queen of the house. Her owner, Barbara, spoiled her rotten. Barbara showered her with gifts, including toy mice and big balls of yarn, her favorite kitty treats, and soft collars in a rainbow of colors.

2   Even though Violet had her own velvety bed, complete with little pillows and blankets, she slept wherever she desired. She curled up on top of the couch or sprawled out in the middle of the living room rug. At night, she always slept with Barbara, right smack in the middle of the bed. One of her favorite places to relax was on her owner's lap. Barbara would stroke the soft fur between her ears, and she would purr contentedly and smile.

3   The only thing that could disturb Violet's peace of mind was a visit from Melrose, the giant orange cat who lived next door. Melrose's owner was away a lot, so Barbara babysat him. Melrose always gobbled down Violet's food as well as his own. He sat in Violet's favorite sunny spot on the windowsill.

4   One day, Violet decided she had had enough of Melrose. When Barbara woke up that morning, she found Melrose in the windowsill. Violet, though, had vanished. She was nowhere to be found. Barbara couldn't account for it. She was frantic with worry, looking in every cabinet and closet, and under every bed and chair. Barbara went door to door, asking neighbors if they had seen her precious cat. No one had seen Violet.

5   Two days later, Barbara still had not found Violet. Melrose's owner came to take Melrose home and to thank Barbara for taking care of him. Barbara had just gone back in her house and closed the door when she recognized a familiar sound. It was Violet meowing at the door.

> **TIP**
>
> When you do not know the meaning of a word, stop and look for clues to help you figure it out.

> **TIP**
>
> How can antonyms help you figure out the meaning of vanished?

6   Barbara opened the door and joyfully scooped up Violet, who purred loudly. Violet had been hiding in the garage, and she was hungry, cold, and tired. She was glad to be home again sitting in Barbara's warm lap and ruling the roost once more.

TIP

If a group of words like ruling the roost does not make sense, use clues from the story to help you figure out the meaning of the expression.

1   **Read the sentence from Paragraph 2.**

Barbara would stroke the soft fur between her ears, and she would purr <u>contentedly</u> and smile.

What is the meaning of <u>contentedly</u> in the sentence above?

A   angrily

B   happily

C   impatiently

D   loudly

TIP

How does Violet act when she is petted? These clues tell you what contentedly means.

2   **Read the sentence from Paragraph 4.**

Violet, though, had <u>vanished</u>.

What is the meaning of the word <u>vanished</u>?

F   arrived

G   disappeared

H   discovered

J   observed

1   Ⓐ Ⓑ Ⓒ Ⓓ
2   Ⓕ Ⓖ Ⓗ Ⓙ

GO ON ▶

3 Read the dictionary entry for the word <u>account</u>.

> **account** \ ə-kau-nt\ *verb* **1.** To provide an explanation.
> **2.** To analyze. *noun* **3.** A record of debt and credit.
> **4.** Value, importance.

Read the sentence from Paragraph 4.

> *Barbara couldn't <u>account</u> for it.*

**Which definition of the word <u>account</u> is used in the
sentence above?**

A   definition 1

B   definition 2

C   definition 3

D   definition 4

> **TIP**
>
> The definition you choose
> should be the same part of
> speech as the original word.

4 Which word from Paragraph 5 helps the reader
understand the meaning of the word <u>recognized</u>?

F   back

G   closed

H   familiar

J   sound

> **TIP**
>
> Eliminate any answer
> choices that do not help you
> understand the meaning of
> <u>recognized</u>.

3 Ⓐ Ⓑ Ⓒ Ⓓ

4 Ⓕ Ⓖ Ⓗ Ⓙ

STOP

Conclusions and Generalizations

Skill Overview

In *I Could Do That!,* Esther invited influential people to her house and treated them well. She agreed with what they said. However, the author never directly states that Esther invited them so that she could convince them that women should get the right to vote. The reader can figure it out, though, using clues in the story. Esther saw a sign explaining that male citizens 21 and older could vote in Wyoming Territory for the first time. This and other clues help the reader conclude that Esther wants to get the men to help women gain the right to vote.

Authors do not always tell every detail. Instead, they give clues and let readers figure things out. When you use clues to figure out something that is not directly stated, you **draw a conclusion**. You can also **make a generalization** about what you read. A generalization states an overall truth that applies to the whole selection.

When you draw a conclusion or make a generalization, you must explain why you think as you do. Suppose that you tell a friend that the bus will come in five minutes. She might ask, "How do you know?" Maybe you have a schedule or rode that bus before. Either way, you have a reason for knowing and can support your idea.

The same is true when you give ideas about what you read. You use the events and other details in the passage to support your conclusions and generalizations.

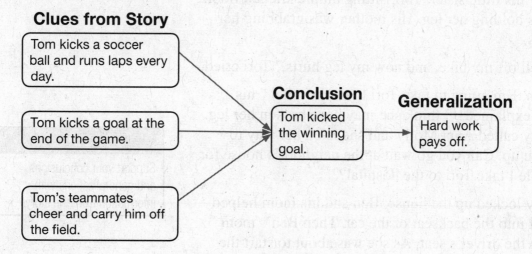

GO ON ▶

Skill Practice

Directions   Read the story. Then answer Numbers 1 through 6.

Only One Choice

1   Ben had dreamed all his life about river rafting. His Aunt Molly went river rafting every chance she could get and described the thrill she felt riding the rough currents. She promised Ben that as soon as he was old enough to use an oar to wrestle through the water, she would take him with her.

2   That day had arrived! Ben had told everyone he knew that he was going, including his little sister Tori, who listened intently as he described the roaring rapids, her eyes wide. Ben told Tori that when she was old enough, they could all go on a river rafting adventure together. Ben took Tori on other adventures, like fishing trips to the creek. He showed her how to put the bait on a hook and reel in a fish.

3   On the big day, Ben was packing when he heard his mom yell, "Ben! Come quickly!" He raced downstairs and saw his little sister, Tori, sitting on the kitchen floor. She was holding her leg. His mother was grabbing her car keys.

4   "I fell off my bike, and now my leg hurts," Tori cried.

5   "Ben, I'm going to take Tori to the hospital," his mother explained. "I think she may have broken her leg. I already called Aunt Molly and she is on her way to pick you up. Can you go wait at the neighbor's house for her while I take Tori to the hospital?"

6   They locked up the house. Ben and his mom helped Tori get into the backseat of the car. Then Ben's mom got into the driver's seat. As she was about to start the engine, Ben made a decision.

7   "Mom, wait a second."

8   Ben got in the back seat next to Tori and said, "I think this is enough excitement for me today."

TIP

The title often gives a clue about important events in a story. Reread it when you draw a conclusion or make a generalization.

TIP

The key events and facts in a story can support your conclusions. Review the facts and events you have read about so far.

TIP

Support your conclusions and generalizations with information from the story.

---

1 What conclusion can you draw from the meaning of the title "Only One Choice"? Give details from the story to support your answer.

_____

_____

_____

_____

2 What conclusion can you draw about Ben's relationship with his sister Tori? Give <u>two</u> details from the story to support your answer.

_____

_____

_____

_____

3 Can you generalize that Ben likes to spend time outdoors based on the story? Give <u>two</u> details from the story to support your answer.

_____

_____

_____

_____

GO ON ▶

Name _____ Date _____

4 What generalization can you make about Ben's character? Give <u>three</u> details from the story to support your answer.

_____

_____

_____

_____

_____

5 Do you think Ben will skip the rafting trip to be with his sister? Give <u>two</u> details from the story to support your answer.

_____

_____

_____

_____

_____

6 What generalization can you make from this story? Give <u>two</u> details from the story to support your answer.

_____

_____

_____

_____

_____

STOP

80

Prefixes

Skill Overview

Many words in English begin with groups of letters called prefixes. A **prefix** can be attached to the beginning of a word. Though prefixes are not usually words themselves, they do have meanings. Adding a prefix changes the meaning of the base word or the root word. You saw a few words with prefixes in the passage *The Ever-Living Tree*.

Three common prefixes include *pre-, inter-,* and *ex-*.

The prefix *pre-* means "before." Examples of words with this prefix include:

- *prehistory*. This word means *before history*, or *before people started recording what happened in the world*.
- *pregame*. This word usually refers to programs and events that take place *before a game*.
- *predict*. This word comes from *pre-* and the root word *dict*. This root *dict* means *say* or *tell*, so to *predict* is to *say before*, or tell what will happen in the future.

The prefix *inter-* usually means "between" or "among." Examples include:

- *international*. A nation is a country, so *international* means *between countries* or *having to do with more than one country*.
- *interaction*. An *interaction* is an *activity* or *communication between or among* two or more people.

Finally, the prefix *ex-* often means "out" or "outside." An example is:

- *exclude*. The prefix *ex-* means *out*, and the root word *clude* means to shut or close. To *exclude* someone is to *shut them out* or *leave them out*.

Sometimes the meaning of a word with one of these prefixes is easy to see. Sometimes you have to think a bit to see how the prefix affects the word's meaning. If a meaning isn't obvious, context clues can help you discover exactly what the word means.

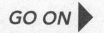

GO ON ▶

Name _____ Date _____

Skill Practice

Directions   Read the story. Then answer Numbers 1 through 4.

Freddy's Future Home

1   "I have a question for you," said Freddy to his best friend, Micah. The boys were on the bus heading to their after-school art class. "If you could live anywhere at all—I mean, *anywhere*—where would it be?"

2   Micah wrinkled his nose. "That's a good question," he began. "I like the beach, and I like the mountains, but if I could live anywhere in the entire world—"

3   "Well, see, I wouldn't live *in* the world," Freddy said, interrupting Micah as the bus stopped for a traffic light. "I would live in space, in a space colony on Mars, or on Neptune, or maybe on Jupiter. That would be amazingly cool—don't you think it would be exciting?"

4   "Um—" Micah began.

5   "I know there's no oxygen on Mars," Freddy said, "but that shouldn't be a problem. All you need to do is build a huge dome, and then you prepare for people to live there by filling the dome with regular air. The roof and the walls of the dome keep the oxygen inside so that people can inhale and exhale just the way we do on Earth."

6   "Well, the problem is—" said Micah.

7   "Jupiter would be a lot tougher than Mars, I admit it," said Freddy, paying no attention to his friend. "Jupiter is made out of hot gas and doesn't have any land at all. You'd have to have a dome that could float extremely well on the vapor." Freddy pointed at a truck parked at a nearby intersection. "But they can build vehicles and computer chips and other complicated things, right?"

8   Micah started to speak, but Freddy just kept going. "So why couldn't they make a dome that wouldn't be affected by gas?" he demanded. "You just have to take a few precautions to make sure it wouldn't burn up or anything."

9   "Freddy," Micah said, "I think—"

> **TIP**
>
> The word interrupt begins with the prefix *inter-*. How does knowing the meaning of the prefix help you understand the meaning of the word?

> **TIP**
>
> Look for words with prefixes that mean before, between, or out.

> **TIP**
>
> What words in these paragraphs have prefixes? What do the prefixes mean? What do the words mean?

10   "I know what you're going to say, Micah," Freddy
said with a grin. "You're going to say it's impossible to
get to Jupiter. That's true now, but by the time we grow
up interplanetary travel will be real. There'll be rockets
going from Mercury to Saturn almost every day, and it
won't take more than a few weeks to get from here to
Jupiter."

11   Micah rolled his eyes. "Listen, Freddy—" he began.

12   "See, the problem with you, Micah, is that you don't
think big," said Freddy, punching his friend lightly
on the arm. "All you dream about is living on a beach
somewhere and climbing mountains in your spare time,
but I think big—all the way to Jupiter!" He pumped his
fist. "Jupiter, here I come!" he sang. "I'll send you a
postcard when I get there."

13   "That may be quite a while," Micah said. He grinned
and elbowed his friend in the ribs, then pointed to a
nearby street sign. "We passed the stop for art class
almost a mile ago, but you were too busy talking to
notice. If you don't know when to exit the bus, I don't
see how you can ever take a trip to Jupiter!"

1   **Read the sentence from Paragraph 5.**

*"The roof and the walls of the dome keep the
oxygen inside so that people can inhale and
exhale just the way we do on Earth."*

**What is the meaning of <u>exhale</u> in the sentence
above?**

A   breathe in

B   breathe out

C   jump up and down

D   throw things away

TIP

Think about the prefix *ex-*.
Also think about what Freddy
is discussing when he uses
this word.

---

1 Ⓐ Ⓑ Ⓒ Ⓓ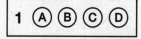

2 Which word from the story means "a place where two or more streets come together"?

F attention

G extremely

H intersection

J vapor

TIP

You may want to reread Paragraph 7. Look for prefixes and clue words to help you.

3 Which words in the story suggest doing something <u>before</u> doing something else?

A exit, exciting

B interrupt, inhale

C punching, elbowed

D prepare, precautions

TIP

What prefix means <u>before</u>? Go back and read the sentences with these words to make sure the meaning makes sense.

4 Read the sentence from Paragraph 10.

"That's true now, but by the time we grow up interplanetary travel will be real."

What is the meaning of <u>interplanetary travel</u> in the sentence above?

F going between two or more planets

G going to the center of Mars or Jupiter

H going from one city or town to another

J going from the North Pole to the South Pole

2 (F) (G) (H) (J)

3 (A) (B) (C) (D)

4 (F) (G) (H) (J)

STOP

Language

Skill Overview

You can use adjectives and adverbs to make your writing clearer and more interesting. An **adjective** is a word that describes a noun or pronoun. Adjectives tell *what kind*, *how many*, and *which one*. Tall, stormy, noisy, and crowded are examples of adjectives.

An **adverb** tells about a verb. An adverb tells how, when, or where. Quickly, happily, and recently are examples of adverbs.

Commas tell readers when to stop and pause. We use commas in different ways when writing.

Separate words in a series	The flag is red, white, and blue.
Separate a date and its year	July 22, 2013
Separate a city and state names	Nashville, TN
Following the greeting and closing of a friendly letter	Dear Rudy, Love, Anna

An **abbreviation** is a shortened form of a word. Many abbreviations begin with a capital letter and end with a period. Abbreviations can be used in addresses to write street names and state names:

Street	*St.*	Avenue	*Ave.*	Road	*Rd.*
Tennessee	*TN*	New York	*NY*	Texas	*TX*

Abbreviations can be used to write days and months:

Monday	*Mon.*	Tuesday	*Tues.*	Friday	*Fri.*
January	*Jan.*	March	*Mar.*	December	*Dec.*

Abbreviations can also be used for people:

Mister	*Mr.*	Doctor	*Dr.*	Senior	*Sr.*

GO ON ▶

Name _____ Date _____

Skill Practice

Directions   Read and answer Numbers 1 through 3.

1   Choose the sentence that uses commas correctly.

   A   Tamika has history, English, and, science classes today.

   B   Tamika has history English and science classes today.

   C   Tamika has history, English, and science, classes today.

   D   Tamika has history, English, and science classes today.

2   Read the sentence.

> *Of the three mountains, Rob climbed the one with the <u>highly peak</u>.*

What is the correct way to write the underlined part of the sentence?

   F   mostly high peak

   G   higher peak

   H   highest peak

   J   correct as is

3   Read the sentence.

> *I have an appointment with <u>Doct. Richards</u> today.*

What is the correct way to write the abbreviation for the underlined name?

   A   Dr. Richards

   B   Dt. Richards

   C   Do. Richards

   D   Dc. Richards

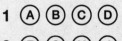

1 Ⓐ Ⓑ Ⓒ Ⓓ
2 Ⓕ Ⓖ Ⓗ Ⓙ
3 Ⓐ Ⓑ Ⓒ Ⓓ

STOP

Responding to a Prompt

Skill Overview

Sometimes you will be asked to respond to a **writing prompt**. The prompt will tell you what kind of writing to do. Before you begin to write, read the prompt twice to make sure you understand it.

Step 1: Planning Your Writing

Think about the kind of writing you will do. For example, the word <u>explain</u> is a clue that you will be writing nonfiction. The words <u>character</u> or <u>setting</u> will help you know that you will be writing a kind of narrative. As you write, keep thinking about the kind of writing the prompt is asking for.

Once you know the kind of writing to do, you need to plan and organize it. Lists, word webs, and freewrites can help you come up with ideas. Story maps and idea-support maps can help you organize what you want to say.

Step 2: Writing a First Draft

You can use the ideas in your graphic organizer or freewrite to write a first draft. For this step, you should not worry about perfect sentences. This is when you should develop your topic and connect your ideas. Consider a beginning, a middle, and an ending for fiction or an introduction, a body, and a conclusion for nonfiction. Remember to write in your own voice.

Step 3: Revising Your Writing

When you revise, you make changes to improve your first draft. You make your writing clearer and more interesting by adding or removing words or details or by changing the order of your sentences. Make sure your writing stays on topic.

Step 4: Editing Your Writing

The editing step is when you correct any spelling or grammar errors you may have made. If you have an editing checklist, now is the time to use it.

Step 5: Writing a Final Draft

The last step is writing your final draft. During this step, you rewrite your paper and put in all the changes you made during the revising and editing steps. Also, make sure your work is neat and written in a handwriting that everyone can read.

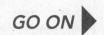

GO ON ▶

Writing to Inform

A writing prompt tells you what to write. One type of writing you may be asked to do is informational. It might be instructions, a description, a report, or an explanation.

Directions   Read the prompt.

Writing Situation: Most people think about a job or career they might want someday in the future.

Directions for Writing: Before you begin writing, think about a career you would like to have.

Now write an essay telling about the job and what about it interests you.

Planning Page

Directions   Use this space to plan your writing. Write your response on your own sheet of paper.

_____

_____

_____

_____

_____

_____

_____

STOP

Reading/Language Arts Practice Test

Part 1

Directions   Read the story. Then answer Numbers 1 through 6.

Mystery Maps

1   Jayla woke up on a sunny Saturday morning, but she did not feel like getting out of bed. She had her own room now and didn't have to share with her pesky little brother, so what was the problem? Jayla's family had moved all the way across the country five weeks ago, and making new friends at school was turning out to be harder than she thought it would be.

2   The move had come in the middle of the year, so the kids at school already had their friends. They weren't looking to make new ones. Since she was the odd one out, they hadn't given her much of a chance. They weren't mean or anything; they just sort of ignored her.

3   Jayla was thinking about her old friends when her mom called her down to breakfast. Jayla was about to say that she didn't want anything when her mom surprised her by saying, "Come down. There's something for you under the door."

4   An envelope with Jayla's name on it had been found by the door with the morning newspaper. Confused, and a little bit excited for the first time in a while, Jayla ripped it open and found a strange piece of paper inside. It was torn at the edges and had dotted lines and squiggly shapes. She didn't know what to make of it.

5   Jayla's brother said, "It looks like some kind of map of our neighborhood."

6   "You're right," replied Jayla. "There's a big X on it where it looks like the park should be."

7   "What else do you see?" Mom asked.

8   Jayla looked more carefully. "It shows a time, 12:00 P.M., and a picture of something that looks like a jar of peanut butter."

9   "Well," Mom said, "you'd better hurry if you're going to make it to the park by 12. And here is a jar of peanut butter, just in case."

10   Jayla dressed quickly, put the peanut butter in her backpack, and jumped on her bike. She arrived at the park just a minute before noon. When she got there, she saw another girl about her age, sitting on a picnic table, looking as confused as she was.

11   "Hi," she said. "I'm Raina. I've seen you at school. You're new around here, right?"

GO ON

12   The girls talked for a few minutes about how they had both received a map under the door that morning and showed up at the park. Jayla brought peanut butter, and Raina had a jar of jelly. They both thought that was bizarre, and it really made them wonder what was going on. As they talked, another girl arrived on a bike with a big smile on her face.

13   "You both made it!" she exclaimed. "Hi Raina. Hi Jayla, I'm Sue. Raina and I are friends at school and I've seen you in class. I thought it would be nice to meet you, so I worked out this unexpected way that we could all get together."

14   Raina laughed. "Sue, I thought I had found a treasure map that was going to lead me to a great treasure!"

15   "It did," said Sue. "A new friend is a true treasure."

16   Sue looked down at the table and saw the peanut butter and jelly. As she opened her backpack, she said, "I see you figured out the clues about what to bring. I brought the bread!" Sue, Raina, and Jayla made sandwiches together. While they talked during the picnic, Jayla realized that, for the first time since her family had moved, it would be easy to get up for school on Monday.

1   **Read the sentence from Paragraph 12.**

   They both thought that was bizarre, and it really made them wonder what was going on.

   What is a synonym for the word bizarre?

   A exciting

   B sad

   C strange

   D wonderful

2   **Why is the setting of a new town important to the story?**

   F Jayla likes living in her new town.

   G Jayla has her own room in the new house.

   H Jayla received a map under the door.

   J Jayla has trouble making friends in her new school.

3 What happens <u>after</u> Jayla rides her bike to the park?

A She puts a jar of peanut butter into her backpack.

B She meets Raina, a girl from her new school.

C Her mother calls her down for breakfast.

D Her brother tells her that the piece of paper has a map of the neighborhood.

4 How is Jayla's problem solved?

F Jayla's mother tells her they will move back to their old town.

G Jayla realizes that friendship is not important.

H Jayla starts to become friends with Raina and Sue.

J Jayla finally gets to eat a sandwich.

5 Based on what happens in the story, what will <u>most likely</u> happen in the future?

A Jayla will start to enjoy her new town.

B Jayla will have to share a room with her little brother.

C Raina and Sue will ignore Jayla at school.

D Jayla's old friends will visit her.

6 The author <u>most likely</u> wrote this story to

F inform the reader of real events.

G entertain the reader with a story.

H convince the reader to make new friends.

J give facts about making new friends.

GO ON ▶

Directions Emilio wrote this journal entry. It has mistakes. Read the journal entry and answer Numbers 7 through 14.

September 28, 2013

(1) Today I woke up early and jumped out of bed right away. (2) I dressed quickly in shorts, a t-shirt, and my tennis shoes. (3) As soon as I was dressed, I ran downstairs and looked out the front windows. (4) I couldn't wait for my grandma to show up! (5) We were going to go to the zoo. (6) We has enjoyed many other days together. (7) Sinse we always have spectacular outings, I knew today would be just as special.

(8) My mom made me sit down and eat breakfast. (9) I was so excited that I couldn't barely eat nothing. (10) As soon as I heard a car pulling up, I raced to the front door. (11) I yelled, "Mom, Yaya's here!"

(12) After Yaya hugged mom and me, Yaya and I got into the car to begin our day of fun. (13) Sang songs as she drove to the zoo.

(14) At the zoo, I ran to see the snakes first. (15) Afterward, I led Yaya all around the zoo to see tigers, elephants, alligators, polar bears, and many other animals. (16) She didn't seem to like the snakes and alligators, but she liked to watch the polar bears swim.

(17) Then we saw a special performance by a group of actors. (18) They put on plaze about animals, and the play we watched was about snakes. (19) It was really cool!

(20) Finally, Yaya drove me home. (21) Before she left, she pulled a bag from her purse. (22) She had bought me a book about snakes. (23) I thanked her with a big hug. (24) What a great surprise

---

7 **Read the date of the journal entry.**

September 28, 2013

Which is the correct abbreviation for the underlined word?

A Spt.

B Septem.

C Sept.

D Sptm.

8 **What is the correct way to write the date at the top of the entry?**

F   September, 28, 2013

G   September, 28 2013

H   September 28 2013

J   correct as is

9 **Read Sentence 6.**

We has enjoyed many other days together.

Which is the best way to write the underlined part of the sentence?

A   have enjoyed

B   enjoys

C   enjoying

D   have enjoys

10 **Read Sentence 18.**

They put on plaze about animals, and the play we watched was about snakes.

Which is the correct way to write the underlined word?

F   playes

G   plais

H   plays

J   correct as is

GO ON

Name _____ Date _____

11 **Read Sentence 13.**

Sang songs as she drove to the zoo.

What is the correct way to write this as a complete sentence?

A   Sang songs as we drove to the zoo.

B   We sang songs as she drove to the zoo.

C   We singing songs as she drove to the zoo.

D   correct as is

12 **Read Sentence 7.**

Sinse we always have spectacular outings, I knew today would be just as special.

Which underlined word in the sentence is spelled incorrectly?

F   sinse

G   spectacular

H   would

J   special

13 **Read Sentence 9.**

I was so excited that I couldn't barely eat nothing.

Which is the correct way to write the underlined part of the sentence?

A   could barely eat anything

B   could not barely eat nothing

C   couldn't barely eat everything

D   couldn't eat nothing

14 **Read Sentence 24.**

What a great surprise

Which is the best punctuation mark to put at the end of the sentence?

F a comma

G a question mark

H a semicolon

J an exclamation mark

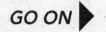

GO ON ▶

Directions   Read the article. Then answer Numbers 15 through 22.

Sunken Treasure

A Voyage from Cuba to Spain

1   It was early July 1715. General Don Juan Esteban de Ubilla had four ships in his New Spain fleet, including the *Urca de Lima*. This ship had a flat bottom and a large cargo area that held crates of chocolate and vanilla. The plan was for Ubilla's fleet to travel from Havana, Cuba, to Spain with the six ships of the Tierra Firme fleet. Together, the fleets would carry their goods, along with $15 million worth of gold and silver, back to Spain. Ubilla knew that many storms hit during the summer, and that this was not a good time to set sail. He also knew that King Philip V of Spain needed the fleets' supplies to pay for his wars. With this in mind, Ubilla decided that the fleets would not wait to make the voyage back to Spain. They left Havana, Cuba, on July 24, 1715.

An Easy Voyage Turns Rough

2   During the first days of the voyage, the two fleets made their way along the east coast of Florida. Ubilla and the fleets' crews were pleasantly surprised by the mild, sunny weather, and they thought they'd have an easy voyage ahead. Soon, however, everything began to change. The waves that gently lapped against their ships turned to large swells. A moist blanket of air filled the sky. Strong winds pushed

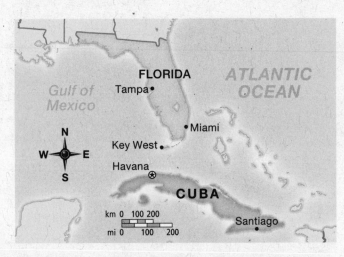

the fleets closer to the shallow reefs of the shoreline. The men knew that the weather would likely get worse, but there was little they could do. On July 31, their fears came true. A huge storm swept through the area, sinking all of the ships in the two fleets.

Recovering the Sunken Treasure

3   News of the sunken ships, and their sunken treasure, spread like wildfire. Boats from Havana and St. Augustine, Florida, quickly made their way to the area. They brought food and other supplies to the survivors. They also brought equipment that would help them recover the sunken treasure. This proved to be a difficult job. Wreckage from the fleets littered over 30 miles of the coastline.

4   The *Urca de Lima* was the only ship that had not completely broken apart. It sank in shallow water, and its flat bottom saved most of its riches from being swept

away. The men went to the *Urca de Lima* first and recovered much of the cargo that she carried. They then moved onto the other ships in the fleet. The men spent several months trying to recover all of the Spanish ships' sunken treasure. By 1716, they gave up, even though half of the treasure still lay on the bottom of the ocean floor.

Rediscovering the *Urca de Lima*

5   Over time, people forgot about the sunken fleets. Then, in 1928, treasure hunters rediscovered the *Urca de Lima*. Like the Spanish sailors before them, the treasure hunters explored the site with the hope that they would find something valuable. For the next 50 years, divers and adventurers from all over the world visited the *Urca de Lima*. Finally, in the 1980s, the state of Florida stopped allowing people to recover items from the sunken ship. Instead, the state opened the *Urca de Lima* to the public. It became Florida's first Underwater Archaeological Preserve.

6   Today, tourists and divers continue to explore the *Urca de Lima*. Its wreckage lies 200 yards offshore near Fort Pierce. As people visit this historic site, they may think about Ubilla's bad decision. But, without that decision, the state of Florida may not have one of its greatest treasures—the only surviving ship from the New Spain fleet of 1715.

15   **Read the sentence from Paragraph 5.**

Then, in 1928, treasure hunters <u>rediscovered</u> the Urca de Lima.

What is the meaning of the underlined word?

A   discovered before

B   discovered again

C   discovered after

D   able to discover

16   **Which section of the article tells about the storm that sank the ships?**

F   A Voyage from Cuba to Spain

G   An Easy Voyage Turns Rough

H   Recovering the Sunken Treasure

J   Rediscovering the *Urca de Lima*

GO ON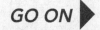

17 **Look at the chart.**

1.	Ubilla decides to make the voyage back to Spain.
2.	The fleets sink.
3.	
4.	The state of Florida opens the *Urca de Lima* site to the public.

Which event belongs in the empty box?

A The fleets leave from Havana, Cuba.

B The fleets travel along the east coast of Florida.

C People recover cargo items from the *Urça de Lima*.

D The state of Florida opens an Underwater Archaeological Preserve.

18 **If a reader wants to see other maps of Cuba and Florida, the best reference to use is**

F a dictionary.

G an encyclopedia.

H an atlas.

J a thesaurus.

19 **Why was it so difficult to recover the sunken treasure?**

A The large storms kept coming.

B The wreck covered more than thirty miles of coast line.

C Too many people were searching.

D Many treasure hunters just gave up.

20 The <u>best</u> source in which to find information about Don Juan Esteban de Ubilla would be a

F Web site titled *Kings and Queens of Spain*.

G journal titled *Modern Spanish Life*.

H picture book titled *All About Ships*.

J book titled *Spanish Generals of the 1700s*.

21 Logan is doing a report about the *Urca de Lima*. Which source could <u>not</u> be used in the early 1900s to research the information for this report?

A a book about the *Urca de Lima*

B an online encyclopedia article about the *Urca de Lima*

C a newspaper article about the *Urca de Lima*

D a letter written by someone who tried to recover treasure from the *Urca de Lima*

22 Read the sentence from Paragraph 3.

They also brought equipment that would help them <u>recover</u> the sunken treasure.

In this sentence, the word <u>recover</u> means

F to feel better.

G to use again.

H to find something that is lost.

J to place something over another item.

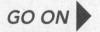
GO ON

Directions   Read the poem. Then answer Numbers 23 through 26.

An Unwelcome Guest

A wild, gray guest blows into town

And people pull their windows down.

Rushing up and down the streets,

She shoves at everyone she meets.

5   They race inside and slam their doors,

As this angry guest shrieks and roars.

"This storm," they cry, "is more than rain!

It has become a hurricane!"

Denied our hospitality,

10   The wild guest tore through our city,

Ripped branches off the sides of trees

And flung them on the street like skis.

Her greenish clouds swirled until they burst.

Her manners were the very worst!

15   Rain poured down like water from a faucet.

Streets were streams, and if your car was there, you lost it.

After putting out every city light

And keeping us awake all night,

The storm blew out of town (she had no bags to pack)

20   But what a mess she left! We'll never ask her back.

23 In the third stanza, the speaker compares tree branches to

A a wild guest.

B skis.

C a street.

D the city.

24 Read Line 2.

And people pull their windows down.

The underlined words are an example of

F alliteration.

G repetition.

H rhyme.

J simile.

25 Who or what is the "wild, gray guest" in the poem?

A an older person

B a strange traveler

C a car

D a hurricane

26 What is the main idea of the poem?

F The speaker enjoys the wind and rain.

G The speaker is excited about the storm.

H The speaker is fearful and upset about the storm.

J The speaker is glad the storm brought so much rain.

GO ON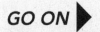

Directions Read the paragraph about the importance of sleep. Then answer Numbers 27 through 30.

Sleep

No one is really sure why the body needs sleep. But people who go without enough sleep for long periods of time become weak and sick. The body has trouble fighting off disease when it is tired. For reasons that are not yet clear, people who sleep too little also tend to gain weight. A possible reason is that one common response to being tired is overeating. Scientists say that sleeplessness can also lead to memory loss and difficulty making decisions. Sleeping is an important part of a healthful life. You should plan your day to give yourself plenty of time to sleep.

27 What would be another good title for this paragraph?

  A   Healthful Living

  B   Don't Lose Sleep

  C   How the Human Body Works

  D   Eating Healthfully

28 Which sentence would make the **best** topic sentence for this paragraph?

  F   Lack of sleep can lead to serious consequences.

  G   Some people stay up way too late.

  H   It is important to eat right every day.

  J   Sleeping too little can make people forgetful.

29 The author **most likely** wrote this paragraph for

   A   people who know why sleep is important.

   B   people who get enough sleep.

   C   scientists who want to know more about sleep.

   D   people who need to know why they need more sleep.

30 The author **most likely** wrote this paragraph to

   F   entertain readers with a story.

   G   explain to readers how to get a good night's rest.

   H   persuade readers to do something that is good for them.

   J   inform readers about a scientific debate.

GO ON ▶

Directions   Read and answer Numbers 31 through 38.

31   **Which sentence is written correctly?**

   A   She walked to school more quick today than yesterday.

   B   She walked to school more quicker today than yesterday.

   C   She walked to school more quickly today than yesterday.

   D   She walked to school quicklier today than yesterday.

32   **Daniel is giving a presentation to a group of students. Which behavior is most appropriate?**

   F   Elise asks Naomi a question while Daniel is talking.

   G   Jonathan listens and takes notes during the presentation.

   H   David prepares for his own speech while Daniel is speaking.

   J   Rachel does her homework during Daniel's presentation.

33   **Read the chart.**

Name	Age	Number of Books Read in March
Dina	10	8
Miguel	11	15
Douglas		12

What belongs in the empty box?

   A   the title for a column

   B   the name of a student

   C   the number of books read

   D   the age of a student

34 Read the table of contents from a book about Tennessee.

Chapter 1	Early History
Chapter 2	The Road to Statehood
Chapter 3	Tennessee in the 21st Century
Chapter 4	Important Cities and Towns

In which chapter would you <u>most likely</u> find information about the largest city in the state?

F Chapter 1

G Chapter 2

H Chapter 3

J Chapter 4

35 Look at the web.

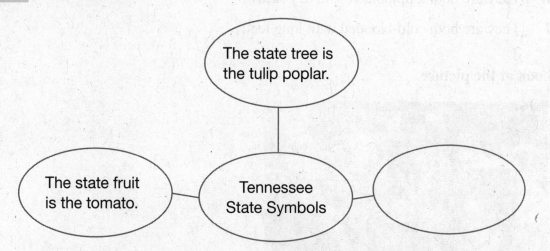

Peter is using this web to plan the first paragraph of his report about Tennessee. Which of these belongs in the empty oval?

A Tulip poplars grow well in the Appalachian Mountains.

B Tennessee is south of Kentucky.

C The state horse is the Tennessee Walking Horse.

D The tulip poplar is also the state tree of Kentucky.

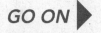

36 **Look at the Venn diagram.**

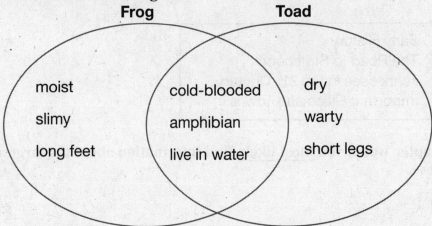

Frog   Toad

moist   cold-blooded   dry
slimy   amphibian   warty
long feet   live in water   short legs

According to the Venn diagram, how are frogs and toads the <u>same</u>?

F They both have short legs.

G They both live in water.

H They are both amphibians with dry skin.

J They are both cold-blooded with long feet.

37 **Look at the picture.**

What is the main idea of this picture?

A A group of people plays in the mud.

B People enjoy the weather on a nice day.

C People work together to plant a tree.

D A group of people digs for treasure.

38 Kyle is doing a report on American culture in the 1960s. Which of these was <u>not</u> available during the 1960s?

F radio

G e-mail

H television

J newspaper

STOP

Part 2

Directions   Read the story. Then answer Numbers 39 through 45.

A Different Kind of Friday

1   Friday morning, the classroom was filled with outdoor tools. There were shovels, rakes, and hoes. The activity table had a box of garden gloves and small digging tools. There were also pinecones and a jar of peanut butter.

2   Aisha was the first student to enter the room that morning. She said to Mr. Agawa, "I have an idea how the tools and gloves might go together, but how do pinecones and peanut butter fit in this group?"

3   Her teacher grinned as he answered, "Don't worry, it will all make sense later."

4   Aisha heard a noise in the hallway and looked out. She was surprised to see Caleb and José pulling a wagon down the hall. Inside the wagon were heavy bags of rocks and planting soil.

5   As the boys pulled the wagon inside the classroom, José said, "Here are the bags you asked us to get from the back of your truck."

6   "What are these for?" asked Caleb. Mr. Agawa only grinned and directed the boys to the spot where he wanted the wagon.

7   Soon, the classroom was full of students. Mr. Agawa pointed out that today was the last Friday in April. It was the day when Arbor Day is celebrated in the United States. He told the students that it is common to plant a tree on that day. Mr. Agawa told his students that they were going to plant three small trees.

8   Mr. Agawa said that in his home country of Japan, the day is called Greenery Day, one of his favorite days. It is held on May 4. There, as in the United States, the day is celebrated by planting trees.

9   Mr. Agawa took his class outside to the front of the school. The principal was already standing there with three saplings that she bought at a garden center. She said that one day they would grow tall and shade the front of the school.

10   The students worked like ants to plant the trees. They took turns digging the holes and poured rocks into the bottom of each one. Mr. Agawa set a tree into each hole. He held each one straight while students poured the planting soil and lightly patted it down with their hands. The students made sure to fill every hole and pack the soil. This would help the small saplings stand straight as they grew into big trees.

11   When the students went back to the classroom, Aisha asked, "Mr. Agawa, now will you tell us what the pinecones and peanut butter are for?"

12   "Yes, of course," he replied. "We are going to make bird feeders to hang in the large trees behind the school. Just follow the directions on this card."

Pinecone Bird Feeders	
Step 1	Tie a long ribbon around the top of a pinecone for hanging it later.
Step 2	Spread some peanut butter all over the sides of the pinecone.
Step 3	Pour birdseed into a paper plate to cover the plate.
Step 4	Roll the pinecone in the birdseed so the seeds stick to it.
Step 5	Use the ribbon to tie the pinecone to a tree branch.

13   After the students made bird feeders, they hung them in the large trees. A few blue jays and robins flew down and began to peck at the seeds. Aisha now understood the reason for Arbor Day. It is a time to plant new trees and be thankful for older ones.

39   **Read the sentence from Paragraph 10.**

He held each one straight while students poured the planting soil and lightly patted it down with their hands.

Based on the suffix –ly, what does lightly mean?

A   in a way that is light

B   to become light

C   to be light again

D   one who is light

40   **Choose the sentence from the story that best supports the conclusion that Mr. Agawa cares about nature.**

F   The students worked like ants to plant the trees.

G   Mr. Agawa pointed out that today was the last Friday in April.

H   Mr. Agawa said that in his home country of Japan, the day is called Greenery Day, one of his favorite days.

J   Her teacher grinned as he answered, "Don't worry, it will all make sense later."

GO ON

41 **How is the setting important to the story?**

A Aisha, Caleb, and José are in the same class on Fridays.

B It is early in the morning and the classrooms are busy.

C The school principal tells everyone about an important holiday in Japan.

D The students celebrate a special event by going outside during the school day.

42 **At the end of the story, you can conclude that the students <u>most likely</u>**

F did not enjoy planting trees and making bird feeders.

G do not understand why it is important to plant trees.

H recognize the importance of Arbor Day.

J would like to visit Japan.

43 **Which sentence would be <u>best</u> to add to Paragraph 10?**

A It was an unusually hot day.

B They took turns digging the holes and poured rocks into the bottom of each one.

C The large oak trees swayed in the breeze.

D There were many ants crawling around on the ground.

44 **What is the <u>main</u> problem in the beginning of the story?**

F Aisha and her classmates want to know why there are unusual items on the activity table.

G Aisha does not like Mr. Agawa's class.

H The principal will not allow the students to plant trees.

J The students do not know how to make bird feeders.

45 To make a bird feeder, what step comes <u>before</u> spreading peanut butter onto the pinecone?

A   Tie a ribbon around the top of the pinecone.

B   Hang the birdfeeder on a tree.

C   Roll the pinecone in birdseed.

D   Pour birdseed on a plate.

GO ON ▶

Directions   Read the poem. Then answer Numbers 46 through 51.

Sea Star
by Desiya Peterson

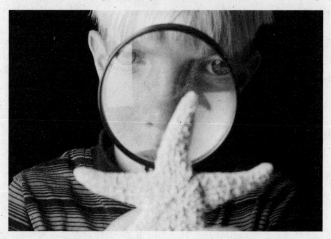

The sea star crawls over the land.
Could it have five arms but not one hand?

It is a star of the ocean,
A wonder of the sea.
5   It is a spiny-skinned creature,
A stanza of poetry.

The sea star has a mouth, but it has no head.
Does it push its stomach from its mouth to be fed?

It is a star of the ocean,
10   A wonder of the sea.
It is a unique creature,
A page out of a fantasy.

One day a predator eats the sea star's arm.
How can the sea star grow it back without a sign of harm?

15   It is a star of the ocean,
A wonder of the sea.
It is a strange creature,
A chapter from a mystery.

46 Which two words from the poem are the most <u>similar</u> in meaning?

    F land, hand

    G wonder, mystery

    H star, ocean

    J chapter, mystery

47 What does the picture show the reader?

    A how the sea star's arm grows back

    B how the sea star is unique

    C that the boy is curious about the sea star

    D that the boy does not like the sea star

48 Which of the following lines from the poem contains a metaphor?

    F The sea star crawls over the land.

    G The sea star has a mouth, but it has no head.

    H It is a strange creature,

    J It is a unique creature, / A page out of a fantasy.

49 Which words from the poem do <u>not</u> compare the sea star to literature?

    A a star of the ocean

    B a stanza of poetry

    C a page out of a fantasy

    D a chapter from a mystery

50 "Sea Star" can be identified as a poem because it has

    F words that describe nature.

    G a beginning and an end.

    H a sentence that compares the sea star to a stanza.

    J lines that end with rhyming words.

GO ON

51 The author **most likely** wrote "Sea Star" to

   A teach readers about fantasy and mystery books.

   B persuade readers to collect sea stars.

   C entertain readers with thoughts about sea stars.

   D explain how sea stars and poets are alike.

Directions   Read the article. Then answer Numbers 52 through 55.

Power from Wind and Water

1   In the United States, we depend on fossil fuels—fuels that are formed in the earth from plant and animal remains—for most of our energy needs. Fossil fuels include coal and oil, which release harmful gases into the air when burned. We burn them to heat our homes and run our cars. We also burn them to make electricity. We use electricity for lighting, heating, and generating power to run machines.

2   We do not have to depend on fossil fuels to make all of our electrical power, however. We can also get energy from water and wind. Both wind and water are renewable energy sources. Renewable means that we will not use them up because we do not burn them or destroy them to get power from them.

3   Moving water contains energy. We can turn this energy into electricity. One way to do this is by building dams. Dams are strong walls that hold back large amounts of water or control how much water flows in a particular place. When water that has been allowed to collect behind the wall finally gets high enough to go over the dam, it falls with great power. The farther it falls and the more of it there is, the more speed and energy the water has. The powerful moving water runs through pipes to a power station. It makes motors spin inside the power station. The motors then make electricity.

4   Although water power does not pollute the environment, it can have some bad effects. For example, dams can disturb fish by changing their habitats, sometimes causing fish to die. Dams can also put some dry land under water, affecting the habitats of other plants and animals.

5   Wind power is another clean way of making electricity. Getting energy from wind does not pollute the air. We can get power from the wind in much the same way that we get power from water. Wind can make electricity because it is moving. Moving air turns the blades of wind machines. The blades are connected to a drive shaft, which is a long pole that spins when the blades turn. The drive shaft then powers a generator. This generator makes electricity.

6   People often build wind farms, which are places where many wind machines are used together to create energy. Some of the best wind farms are on open, flat land. Others are at the tops of hills or near seashores. Either way, wind is one of the best renewable energy sources.

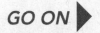

GO ON

52 Which detail from the article supports the idea that water power can have some bad effects?

   F Powerful moving water runs through pipes to a power station.

   G Dams hold back large amounts of water.

   H Moving water contains energy.

   J Dams can disturb fish by changing their habitats.

53 What is <u>one</u> effect of burning fossil fuels to make energy?

   A They release harmful gases into the air.

   B They can be easily renewed.

   C They help conserve water and other resources.

   D They help plant and animal habitats.

54 Which detail from the article is an <u>opinion</u>?

   F Moving water contains energy.

   G Either way, wind is one of the best renewable energy sources.

   H Moving air turns the blades of wind machines.

   J Wind can make electricity because it is moving.

55 Which source would provide the <u>most</u> reliable information on renewable energy?

   A a story about a man chasing windmills

   B a student Web page about a class's science experiment

   C a television commercial about wind power

   D an online encyclopedia

Directions   Read Vivian's speech. Then answer Numbers 56 through 63.

Camping Club

1   Good morning, young campers! My name is Victoria Moore. As many of you know, I am a fourth grade student here at North Hill Elementary School. I am also the student representative of the North Hill Camping Club. Tomorrow afternoon we will leave for the first camping trip of the year. Please listen carefully as I remind you of a few rules that will help every camper be considerate of nature.

2   First, we must all be careful with our food. Food can cause the most trouble with wild animals. Being careful with food can make the difference between a pleasant camping trip and a frightening one. Our teachers and parents will bring food for a cookout, but many of you might want to bring snacks. If you do, ask your parents to help you pack your food in airtight bags. Airtight bags make it harder for animals to smell your food, so they will be less likely to come into the campsite looking for it.

3   Second, we all need to dispose of our trash properly. Do not expect anyone else to clean up after you. When you leave, carry your trash out with you. Don't leave anything behind. Plastic bags, cans, and other pieces of garbage can be harmful to the health of plants and animals. Let's all remind each other to throw away or recycle our items. We are going camping to observe the beauty of nature, not to destroy it.

4   Third, be prepared to have fun! We'll play games, sing songs, and enjoy the great outdoors. We will also spend some time exploring nature. Bring your magnifying glass, pencil, plant guide, and notebook. You can find interesting plants and identify them using your magnifying glass and plant guide. You might even draw the plant in a notebook and record its name. Remember to check your plant guide if you have forgotten what poison ivy and other dangerous plants look like.

5   It's also very important that each of us stays with our group leader. Each group will have a parent or teacher leader. They will help us pitch our tents, cook our food, and participate in all the fun camping activities. Group leaders will track where we are, so sticking with them will keep you from getting lost. Let's show the group leaders that we kids know how to be kind and considerate campers. Don't forget that the group that has the best behavior and wins the most field day events will win special prizes!

6   Thank you for listening, and I'll see you tomorrow. Please pay attention as Ms. Amado assigns our group leaders.

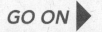

GO ON

56 Victoria is organizing her note cards with the speaking points she will mention in her speech.

Introduction	Remind students to be careful with food.		Remind students to bring a magnifying glass and plant guide.

What information belongs on the blank note card?

F Introduce Ms. Amado to assign group leaders.

G Remind students about the prizes they can win.

H Tell students to clean up their trash.

J Remind students that tomorrow will be the first camping trip of the year.

57 Read the sentence from Paragraph 1.

I am also the student <u>representative</u> of the North Hill Camping Club.

Which source should Victoria use to find a synonym for the underlined word?

A an atlas

B a newspaper

C a thesaurus

D an online encyclopedia

58 Which of the following would <u>best</u> improve Victoria's presentation?

F a digital presentation that lists the rules she mentions

G photographs of the students in the camping club

H an audio recording of an interview with recycling expert

J a map of different campsites in the United States

59 **While listening to Victoria give her speech, the students in the audience should**

   A ask questions before the speech is complete.

   B sit quietly and pay close attention.

   C find a better place to sit if it is hard to see.

   D watch the teacher to know when the speech is over.

60 **Read the sentence from Paragraph 5.**

> *Group leaders will* <u>*track*</u> *where we are, so sticking with them will keep you from getting lost.*

What is the meaning of the underlined word in the sentence above?

   F to follow a course or trail

   G footprints made by animals

   H a line of rails

   J a place to go running

61 **Which sentence from the speech** <u>**best**</u> **shows that it is written for a young audience?**

   A Second, we all need to dispose of our trash properly.

   B We will also spend some time exploring nature.

   C My name is Victoria Moore.

   D Let's show the group leaders that we kids know how to be kind and considerate campers.

GO ON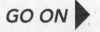

62 Read the analogy.

Harmful is to *dangerous* as *considerate* is to _____.

Which word from the speech best completes the analogy?

F interesting

G kind

H participate

J frightening

63 What is the **best** summary for the speech?

A Students need to learn how to clean up after themselves while camping.

B A new camping club will help students enjoy nature.

C Everyone should follow the rules during tomorrow's camping trip.

D Airtight bags make it harder for animals to smell your food.

Directions Mia wrote the following rough draft of a biography for class. It contains mistakes. Read the report and answer Numbers 64 through 70.

Mahalia Jackson

1 Mahalia Jackson was born October 26 1911, in New Orleans, Louisiana. Mahalia, who's grandfather was a slave, was raised by her aunt. Mahalia loved music as a child, and she heard hymns, jazz, and the blues all around her when she was growing up.

2 In 1928, Mahalia moved to Chicago to find new opportunities. _____, she began singing in church choirs. By the 1930s, Mahalia is becoming well known as a gospel singer. By the 1950s, she was singing on radio and TV shows. Mahalia died of heart failure. As the years went on, her popularity continued to grow.

3 In August of 1963, Dr. Martin Luther King, Jr. asked Mahalia to sing at the March on Washington, right before his famous "I Have a Dream" speech. Writing about gospel music in her autobiography, Mahalia said, "It will last as long as any music because it is sung straight from the human heart." At the march, she sang for a crowd of 250,000 people. There are not many singers as loved and honored as Mahalia.

---

64 **Read these sentences from Paragraph 2.**

In 1928, Mahalia moved to Chicago to find new opportunities. _____, she began singing in church choirs.

Which is the best word to add on the blank space?

F Soon

G Although

H In conclusion

J Before

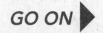

GO ON

65 **Which sentence does not belong in Paragraph 2?**

A In 1928, Mahalia moved to Chicago to find new opportunities.

B By the 1950s, she was singing on radio and TV shows.

C Mahalia died of heart failure.

D As the years went on, her popularity continued to grow.

66 **Read the sentence from Paragraph 1.**

Mahalia, who's grandfather was a slave, was raised by her aunt.

Which is the correct way to write the underlined word?

F whoose

G whose

H who is

J correct as is

67 **Read the sentence from Paragraph 2.**

By the 1930s, Mahalia is becoming well known as a gospel singer.

Which is the best way to correct this sentence?

A By the 1930s, Mahalia becoming well known as a gospel singer.

B By the 1930s, Mahalia have become well known as a gospel singer.

C By the 1930s, Mahalia was becoming well known as a gospel singer.

D By the 1930s, Mahalia had becoming well known as a gospel singer.

68 **Which of these words from the report is a compound word?**

F becoming

G singing

H opportunities

J grandfather

69 Read these sentences from Paragraph 3.

1. In August of 1963, Dr. Martin Luther King, Jr. asked Mahalia to sing at the March on Washington, right before his famous "I Have a Dream" speech.

2. Writing about gospel music in her autobiography, Mahalia said, "It will last as long as any music because it is sung straight from the human heart."

3. At the march, she sang for a crowd of 250,000 people.

Choose the <u>best</u> order for these sentences.

A 3, 1, 2

B 1, 3, 2

C 2, 3, 1

D 3, 2, 1

70 Read the sentence from Paragraph 1.

Mahalia Jackson was born October 26 1911, in New Orleans, Louisiana.

Which is the <u>best</u> way to correct this sentence?

F Mahalia Jackson was born October, 26, 1911, in New Orleans, Louisiana.

G Mahalia Jackson was born October, 26 1911, in New Orleans, Louisiana.

H Mahalia Jackson was born October 26, 1911, in New Orleans, Louisiana.

J Mahalia Jackson was born October 26, 1911, in New Orleans Louisiana.

GO ON

Directions   Read and answer Numbers 71 through 75.

71   **Read the statement below.**

Last year, joined the chorus.

Which is the <u>best</u> way to make this a complete sentence?

A   I joined last year the chorus.

B   Joined the chorus last year.

C   I last year joined the chorus.

D   Last year, I joined the chorus.

72   **Read the statement below.**

The black cat with green eyes.

Which is the correct way to complete the sentence?

F   The black cat with long whiskers and green eyes.

G   The black cat with green eyes quickly.

H   The black cat with green eyes ran quickly.

J   The black cat with green eyes and long tail.

73   **Choose the sentence that uses commas correctly.**

A   Jenny brought markers crayons, and paper to school.

B   Jenny brought markers, crayons, and paper to school.

C   Jenny brought markers crayons and, paper to school.

D   Jenny brought markers crayons and paper to school.

Name _____ Date _____

74 **Read the sentence.**

Kara does not want to miss the class field trip.

What is the correct way to write the underlined words as a contraction?

F don't

G do'nt

H does'nt

J doesn't

75 **A type of story that is usually written to teach a moral, or lesson, is a**

A tall tale.

B biography.

C personal narrative.

D fable.

STOP

Writing Practice Test

Writing to Narrate

Directions   Read the prompt.

> **Writing Situation**: Sometimes it is fun to imagine what it would be like to have a special power.
>
> **Directions for Writing**: Before you begin writing, think about what kind of special power you would want.
>
> Now write a story about what you would do if you had that special power.

Directions   Use this space to plan your writing. Write your response on your own sheet of paper.

_____

_____

_____

_____

_____

_____

_____

STOP

Writing Practice Test

Writing to Inform

Directions Read the prompt.

> **Writing Situation**: Most people have a favorite sport they like to watch or play.
>
> **Directions for Writing**: Before you begin writing, think about the sport you most like to watch or play.
>
> Now write to explain the rules of how to play that sport.

Directions Use this space to plan your writing. Write your response on your own sheet of paper.

_____

_____

_____

_____

_____

_____

_____

STOP

Name _____ Date _____

Writing Practice Test

Writing Opinions

Directions   Read the prompt.

> **Writing Situation**: Everyone lives in a community, but some people think their community could be even better.
>
> **Directions for Writing**: Before you begin writing, think about what could make your community better.
>
> Now write to explain what you think should be done in your community to make it better.

Directions   Use this space to plan your writing. Write your response on your own sheet of paper.

_____

_____

_____

_____

_____

_____

_____

STOP

Name _____ Date _____

Constructed Response

Directions   Read the article. Then answer Numbers 1 through 4.

Tell the World

1   The planet is inhabited by many people. Each person shares a responsibility for it. What can a person do if he or she finds something that needs to be changed in how people treat the planet or each other?

2   Severn Suzuki was a 12-year-old girl who lived in Vancouver, Canada. Severn had always enjoyed nature. She loved going camping and fishing. One day she went fishing with her dad and learned that the fish were full of cancers.

3   Severn began to worry about the environment. She worried about plants and animals. She also worried about other problems that the world faced, such as children who were going hungry. Severn knew she had to do something.

4   She became a member of the Environmental Children's Organization (ECO). This group of 12- and 13-year-olds from Canada wanted to stop the destruction of the environment and make the world a better place. Group members wanted to keep the world safe for future generations.

5   The group raised money to travel 6,000 miles (9,654 kilometers) to the Earth Summit in Rio de Janeiro, Brazil. Members planned to speak before the United Nations Conference on Environment and Development.

6   More than 100 leaders and members of environmental organizations were at this meeting. They wanted to figure out how to save plants and animals. Many plants and animals were disappearing and in danger of becoming extinct.

7   Severn Suzuki was one of the four children who spoke at the conference. In her speech, she shared her biggest fears:

8   "Losing my future is not like losing an election or a few points on the stock market. I am here to speak for all generations to come.

9   I am here to speak on behalf of the starving children around the world whose cries go unheard.

10   I am here to speak for the countless animals dying across this planet because they have nowhere left to go. We cannot afford to be unheard.

11   I am afraid to go out in the sun now because of the holes in the ozone. I am afraid to breathe the air because I don't know what chemicals are in it.

GO ON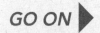

Name _____   Date _____

12   I used to go fishing in Vancouver with my dad until just a few years ago when we found the fish full of cancers. And now we hear about animals and plants going extinct every day—vanishing forever.

13   In my life, I have dreamt of seeing the great herds of wild animals, jungles and rain forests full of birds and butterflies, but now I wonder if they will even exist for my children to see.

14   Did you have to worry about these little things when you were my age?

15   All this is happening before our eyes, and yet we act as if we have all the time we want and all the solutions.

16   I'm only a child and I don't have all the solutions, but I want you to realize neither do you!"

17   She begged the leaders, "If you don't know how to fix it, please stop breaking it!" Severn reminded them, "We are all in this together and should act as one single world working toward one single goal."

18   Many people were moved by Severn Suzuki's speech. She told the world exactly how she felt. That was the first step to making a difference.

1   **Based on the author's description of Severn Suzuki, what can the reader conclude about Suzuki's personality? Give <u>two</u> details from the article to support your answer.**

_____

_____

_____

_____

Name _____ Date _____

2 What is the meaning of the word <u>environment</u> as it is used in Paragraph 3?

_____

_____

_____

_____

3 Complete the web with <u>one</u> detail from the article.

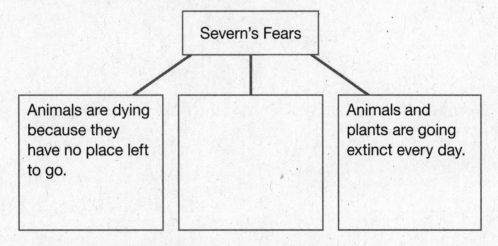

Severn's Fears

Animals are dying because they have no place left to go.

Animals and plants are going extinct every day.

Explain how this detail accurately completes the web.

_____

_____

_____

_____

GO ON ▶

Name _____ Date _____

4 According to the author, what does it take for someone to help the world?

_____

_____

_____

_____

_____

STOP

Constructed Response

Directions   Read the story. Then answer Numbers 1 through 4.

Time Out

1   "Maria, will you play with me?"

2   I glanced up from my book to see my little sister Sasha standing by my chair. Sighing, I shut the book, keeping my thumb between the pages to mark my place. I didn't want to hurt Sasha's feelings, but it was already past four o'clock and I didn't have time.

3   "I'm in the middle of this book, sweetie," I said gently, "and then I have some homework to do before dinner, and I have basketball practice after that. Maybe we can play tomorrow."

4   "I don't want to play with you tomorrow," said Sasha flatly. "I want to play with you *now*."

5   "You could build with your blocks," I suggested. "That's a fun thing to do by yourself." I tried to sound jolly and enthusiastic, but I knew I was fighting a losing battle.

6   "Blocks are boring," said Sasha. "Anyway, the blocks are in time out because I tried to build a tower but it fell down and squished my foot, so I put the blocks in time out, just like Mommy does to me when I do something bad."

7   I had to smile at the idea of putting blocks in time out. Sasha gets put in time out— well, not all the time, but it does happen fairly often, so I guess she knows what it's like.

8   "Maria, I want to play with you," Sasha repeated.

9   I closed my eyes and rubbed my forehead. The trouble with Sasha—well, there are lots of troubles with Sasha, but one is that she doesn't ever believe you when you say no to her, or at least, she doesn't accept it when you say it. Instead, she just stands there asking you again and again until you finally agree to do exactly what she wants.

10   "I really really really really want you to play with me," Sasha said.

11   I glanced down at my book and sighed again. "I guess this can wait while we play for a bit," I said.

12   "We're going to play with my stuffed animals," Sasha explained as I walked into her room.

13   I sat down next to Monkeykins, one of Sasha's favorites. "Let's see what Monkeykins wants to do today."

GO ON ▶

Name _____ Date _____

14 "Oh, you can't play with Monkeykins," Sasha informed me. "She's in time out."

15 I looked quizzically at Sasha. "What did she do to get herself into time out?"

16 "Something *terrible*," Sasha said in a low voice, her eyes as big as dinner plates. "She pulled Elephant's tail."

17 Inside I was laughing, but I pretended to be shocked.

18 "She pulled it," Sasha repeated, "and Elephant cried and I put Monkeykins in time out and she has to stay there until she's ready to behave."

19 "Did you hear what just happened, Maria?"

20 I looked up from the stuffed raccoon I was holding.

21 "Bubbles was being mean to Sparky," Sasha explained sorrowfully. She picked up a stuffed pig and shook her finger in its face. "That was very naughty, Bubbles," she said. "It's not nice to call people nasty names, so I'm going to need to put you in time out."

22 I stifled a laugh. Time out was growing larger and larger every minute; besides Monkeykins, Sasha had put a sheep, a bear, a parrot, a moose, and two rabbits in time out in just the last ten minutes, and now it looked like Bubbles the pig was going to join them. I playfully threw Bubbles into the time-out pile.

23 "Maria! That's not very nice to do to Bubbles," Sasha said seriously. "I'm sorry, but you'll have to go in time out, too."

24 This time I couldn't help laughing out loud. Sasha led me to time out. At least I would get to play with Monkeykins now.

1 **What are Maria's feelings toward Sasha? Give <u>two</u> details from the story to support your answer.**

_____

_____

_____

_____

_____

Name _____ Date _____

2 What does Maria's mother mean when she compares Sasha to rain falling on a rock?

_____

_____

_____

_____

3 What do you learn about Sasha in the story? Give <u>two</u> details from the story to support your answer.

_____

_____

_____

_____

GO ON ▶

Name _____ Date _____

4 Think about the order of events in the story.

Complete the timeline with <u>one</u> detail from the story.

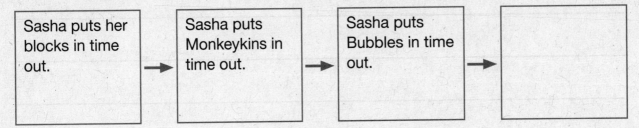

| Sasha puts her blocks in time out. | → | Sasha puts Monkeykins in time out. | → | Sasha puts Bubbles in time out. | → | |

Explain why this detail accurately completes the timeline.

_____

_____

_____

_____

_____

STOP

Constructed Response

Directions Read the article. Then answer Numbers 1 though 4.

Garden Show Opens Soon

1 GREEN VALLEY August 8— In just one short week, our annual Green Valley Amazing Vegetables Garden Show begins. Just like every year, we are looking forward to our favorite Green Valley event. This year's show promises to be better than ever. It will be held on August 15 at the Green Valley City Park.

2 The event will kick off with the Amazing Vegetables Parade. The parade starts at City Hall at 8:00 A.M. and marches on Spring Street to the park. (See schedule of events at the end of this article.) The parade features more than 100 farmers and gardeners pushing wheelbarrows filled with their amazing vegetables. The judges will award a prize for the best-decorated wheelbarrow. The Green Valley High School marching band is also scheduled to appear in the parade, along with several marching scout groups.

3 Morning events include the Tomato and Pepper Contest and the Squash and Onions Contest. Last year, Dr. W. D. Seeds grew the largest tomato ever seen in Green Valley. It weighed in at 8 pounds, 4 ounces. Will anyone tie or break her record this year? Will anyone grow a pepper hotter than Sammy Ortega's winner from last year? Visit the Tomato and Pepper Tent to find out.

4 People visiting the Squash and Onions Tent are in for some grand sights. Last year, it took two people to lift some of the squashes, including—of course—the prizewinner. The biggest onion was nearly the size of a soccer ball! Ribbons will be awarded for the largest squash and onion.

5 Be sure to stop by the baseball field for lunch. Have a slice of vegetable lasagna made by students from Green Valley School. They are going for a world record for the longest dish of lasagna. Iced vegetable drinks and corn on the cob will also be served.

GO ON

Name _____ Date _____

6   The Carrots and Corn Contest will be held in the afternoon, with prizes awarded at 4:00 P.M. The Tanner twins took the prizes last year for the biggest carrot and the biggest ear of corn. One carrot was almost as tall as the twins! Can they do it again? Come see for yourself!

7   Two other events are sure to draw crowds all day. Both the Vegetables-on-View Tent and our own Farmers' Market will be open to the public from 9:00 A.M. until 5:00 P.M. A contest called *That Vegetable Looks Just Like . . .* will invite growers with a good imagination. The contest will be held at the Vegetables-on-View Tent. Last year, Daisy Black grew a pumpkin that looked just like her dog, Spot. Mr. Lee from Lee's Hardware Store grew a potato that looked like Benjamin Franklin. Both won prizes. You never know what will turn up in this popular contest.

8   The Farmers' Market will sell the most amazing vegetables. Most are huge, and all are delicious. Shoppers are advised to bring their wheelbarrows and load up on vegetables. Free delivery is offered for those who buy a truckload.

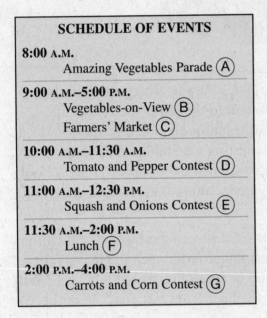

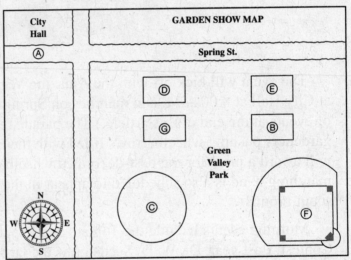

Name _____ Date _____

1 How does the reader know that the author is trying to persuade readers to visit the Garden Show? Give <u>two</u> details from the article to support your answer.

_____

_____

_____

_____

2 How is the information in the article organized?

_____

_____

_____

_____

GO ON ▶

Name _____ Date _____

3 Think about the information provided in the article. Complete the idea support map to support the idea that the Garden Show is full of unusual things to see.

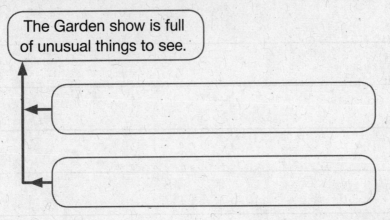

The Garden show is full of unusual things to see.

Explain why these two details accurately complete the idea support map.

_____

_____

_____

_____

_____

4 How could the reader use the information in the text, schedule, and map to plan a visit to the Garden Show?

_____

_____

_____

_____

STOP

Constructed Response

Directions   Read the play. Then answer Numbers 1 through 4.

Lost and Found

Characters:

JON LIU, age 9

ANDREW LIU, age 11

MRS. LIU

BETHANY THOMAS, age 16

MR. THOMAS

SCENE 1

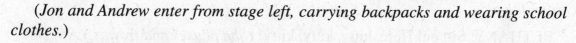

(*Jon and Andrew enter from stage left, carrying backpacks and wearing school clothes.*)

JON: Did you see that kickball game at recess? (*Stops walking and holds up his hand, listening.*) Hold on, did you hear something?

ANDREW: Yeah, it sounded like a bell, and I think it was coming from over here. (*Andrew walks to a bush, reaches behind it, and picks up a kitten with a bell on its collar.*)

JON: What are you doing back there, little guy? (*Takes the kitten from Andrew.*) Andrew, do you think we can keep him? Mom said maybe we could get a cat sometime soon, and I bet that if we ask really, really nicely, she'll say we can have this one!

ANDREW: Let's go home and we can see what she says.

(*Andrew and Jon exit stage right.*)

SCENE 2

(*Jon is sitting on the living room floor, petting the kitten while Andrew watches. Mrs. Liu walks in and jumps, startled.*)

MRS. LIU: Where did that kitten come from?

ANDREW: We found it behind some bushes down at the other end of the street.

JON: (*Jumps up and runs over to his mother, eager.*) Can we keep it?

MRS. LIU: (*Walks over and picks up the kitten, looking thoughtful.*) It has a collar, so that suggests that someone is taking care of it. It probably ran outside and got lost, so I imagine that the owner must be looking for it.

GO ON

Name _____ Date _____

JON: (*Looks disappointed, then perks up.*) But if it turns out that no one is trying to find it, then we can keep it, right?

MRS. LIU: (*Hands the kitten to Jon, who hugs it close.*) Well, let's try to find the owner first. Why don't you boys make posters to put up in the neighborhood? I'll put an advertisement in the newspaper tomorrow, and if no one claims the kitten, then maybe we'll keep it.

ANDREW: I'll get some paper and markers.

SCENE 3

(*The boys are outside finishing up taping a poster to a telephone pole. As they walk away, Bethany and Mr. Thomas walk toward the pole, looking from side to side and calling for a cat.*)

BETHANY: Simon! Here, kitty, kitty, kitty! (*She pauses and frowns.*) Aw, Dad, we'll never find him! I really wish I'd closed the back door!

MR. THOMAS: Well, let's just keep looking. He's probably still nearby. (*Stops in front of the poster and starts to read it.*) Hey, look. "Did you lose a cute little—"

BETHANY: (*She turns to look at the sign and clasps her hands together under her chin.*) Oh, Dad, do you think it might be—

JON (*Starts to speak, then hesitates as Bethany and Mr. Thomas turn to look at him, then starts again*): Um, are you looking for an orange kitten? One that's real nice and doesn't scratch you when you pick him up?

BETHANY: (*Excited.*) Dad, I bet that's Simon!

ANDREW: The kitten was hiding behind some bushes, and we found him when we were walking home. Come on, we'll show you. (*Andrew starts to walk away. Jon doesn't follow, and looks sad.*) Jon, come on! This girl has to be his owner.

JON: (*To Andrew, in a low voice; Bethany is watching them and overhears.*) I bet she really misses her cat, but now I'll never see him again!

BETHANY: We live right in the neighborhood, so you could visit him sometimes. He always needs someone to play with while I do my homework.

JON: Really? Wow! You bet I'll come visit!

(*All walk offstage.*)

Name _____ Date _____

1 What features does this play include that would <u>not</u> be found in a story?

_____

_____

_____

_____

_____

2 Complete the Venn diagram with details from the play. Show how Jon's and Andrew's reactions to the kitten are alike and different.

Jon's Reactions   Andrew's Reactions

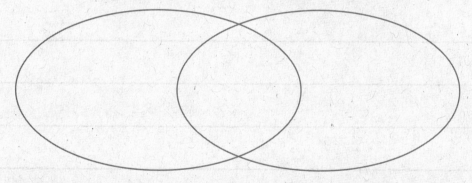

Explain how Jon's and Andrew's reactions to the kitten are alike and different.

_____

_____

_____

_____

_____

GO ON ▶

Name _____ Date _____

3 Suppose you are playing the part of Bethany in a production of "Lost and Found." What emotions would you use while reading your lines in the beginning of Scene 3?

_____

_____

_____

_____

_____

4 What lesson does Jon learn in the play? Give <u>two</u> details from the play to support your answer.

_____

_____

_____

_____

_____

STOP

Constructed Response

Directions Read the articles. Then answer Numbers 1 through 4.

Inventing the Telephone

1   Suppose that you want to talk to your friend who lives across the street without leaving your house. You could yell to your friend, but you would have to yell loudly. On the other hand, you could use the telephone to speak to your friend directly. You could even talk to someone on the other side of the world with a telephone. Where did this powerful machine come from?

2   Today telephones are a part of everyday life. But 150 years ago, no one had ever seen one. People who wanted to send messages over long distances used the telegraph. The telegraph used electricity to send messages. Changes in electric current stood for the letters of the alphabet. Telegraph wires carried messages hundreds or even thousands of miles.

3   Alexander Graham Bell studied how the telegraph worked. From childhood, he was interested in sounds and human speech. His father was a well-known expert on speech, and his mother was unable to hear. As a young man, Bell worked as a teacher for students who were deaf. He worked in his spare time to make a better telegraph.

4   Since more and more telegraph messages were being sent over telegraph wires, Bell wanted to create a new telegraph that could send many messages at the same time. Bell thought that his telegraph would use different pitches of sound to keep the various messages in order.

5   Bell worked with an assistant, Thomas Watson, to perfect his new telegraph. One day, while they worked on their project, Bell made an accidental discovery. He learned that electricity could carry sound directly. He decided to work on a machine that would send the sound of a person's voice from one place to another.

GO ON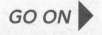

Name _____ Date _____

6   Bell and Watson worked on the telephone for many months. Their basic idea was correct, but they were unable to make the sound easy to understand. Then on February 14, 1876, Bell announced to the U.S. government that he had found a way to send the human voice over wires. But the world's first telephone call happened a few weeks later. Bell made the call on March 10 to his assistant, saying, "Mr. Watson, come here. I want you." That summer, he introduced his new invention to the world at the Philadelphia Centennial Exposition.

1   **What problem did the invention of the telephone help to solve? Give <u>one</u> detail from the article to support your answer.**

_____

_____

_____

_____

2   **What experiences in Alexander Graham Bell's life led him to invent the telephone?**

_____

_____

_____

_____

Name _____ Date _____

Talking on a String

At the Save Our Planet Club, we are always looking for new ways to reuse and recycle everyday materials. Here's a fun way you can reuse cans to make a can telephone.

Materials:

- 2 cans, about the same size, clean and empty; each can has one lid removed
- hammer
- nail
- pencil
- string, 8–10 feet long

What To Do:

1. Gather all your materials. Find an adult who can help you.

2. Place your cans on the ground with the open ends facing down. Mark a spot in the center of each top. Then ask the adult to help you punch a hole through the marked spot with a hammer and a nail in the top of each can.

3. Next push one end of the string through the hole in one of the cans. Use a pencil to push the string through, *not your finger.* Then knot the string firmly inside the can.

4. Push the other end of the same string through the hole in the top of the second can and knot it also. Now you have your can telephone.

Using Your Can Telephone:

To enjoy your telephone, find a friend to use it with. Each of you take one can. Pull the string tightly between you and make sure it does not touch anything. Speak into your can while your friend holds the other can to his or her ear. Then switch roles. Teach others how to make can telephones. It can be fun!

How a Can Telephone Works:

Like a real telephone, your can telephone lets sound waves travel back and forth. Sound travels well through a solid, like your piece of string. When one person speaks into the can, the sound makes the string vibrate. The sound waves travel along the string to the other can telephone. When they reach your friend's ear, he or she can hear what you said. What happens if you pinch the string with your finger? The sound waves are interrupted. They cannot travel past your finger. As a result, your friend will not hear what you said. The sound waves cannot reach the other can.

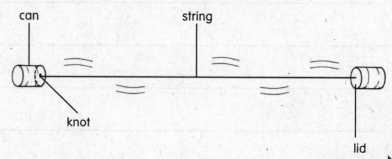

GO ON ▶

Name _____ Date _____

3 Imagine you want to tell a friend how to make a can telephone. Write a few sentences explaining the process in your own words.

_____

_____

_____

_____

_____

4 Complete the Venn diagram with details from the articles. Show how Alexander Graham Bell's first telephone and a can telephone are alike and how they are different.

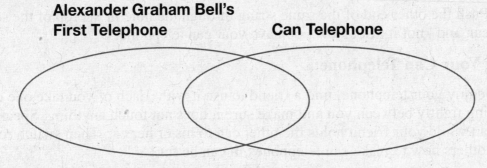

Alexander Graham Bell's
First Telephone   Can Telephone

Explain how the two telephones are alike and how they are different.

_____

_____

_____

_____

STOP

Name _____ Date _____

Constructed Response

Directions   Read the stories. Then answer Numbers 1 through 4.

Opossum and Iguana

1   Long ago, Opossum lived in a Mexican village. Quiet and watchful, she sat all day in a mango tree and saw everything that was going on in the village. The other animals never noticed her or came to visit.

2   Underneath the mango tree lived Iguana. Iguana was the only villager who knew how to make fire from sticks. When the people in the village needed fire for cooking or warmth, they came to him.

3   One night Opossum heard Iguana say loudly to his wife, "I should be the ruler of this village because I am the only one who can make fire. I will show all the villagers how much they need me!" Then he took all the fire and climbed to the top of a cliff.

4   The next morning the villagers cried out, "There is no fire!"

5   "Iguana carried it up the cliff to the sky," explained Opossum.

6   The villagers discussed who should go to get back the fire. They all agreed that Opossum should go.

7   So Opossum scrambled up the cliff. At the top she found Iguana.

8   "I suppose you've come to steal my fire," said Iguana.

9   Opossum said, "You are too smart for me, Iguana, and I could never steal fire from you."

10   Iguana's chest puffed up, and he began to tell boastful stories about himself. On and on he went, telling one story after another until Opossum said, "You look tired."

11   "I *am* tired," Iguana yawned, and he turned away and fell asleep. As he did, Opossum reached into the fire, wrapped her tail around a burning branch, and threw it over the edge of the cliff to the villagers below. In the process, all the hair on her tail burned away.

12   "You thief!" Iguana shouted, waking up and seeing what she was doing.

GO ON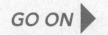

Name _____ Date _____

13   Frightened, Opossum curled up and pretended to be dead. Iguana poked her to see if she was really dead. His poke was so strong that Opossum fell over the side of the cliff. Fortunately, Raven caught her.

14   Now everyone in the village had fire. They no longer had to ask Iguana when they needed fire for cooking or warmth. Still, to this day, Opossum has a hairless tail, which reminds everyone of how she brought fire to the people. And if Opossum is in danger, she continues to curl up into a ball and pretend to be dead.

1   How does Opossum feel at the beginning of the story? Give <u>one</u> detail from the story to support your answer.

_____

_____

_____

_____

2   How did Opossum get the fire from Iguana?

_____

_____

_____

_____

How I Lost My Tail, by Mr. B. Bear

1   This is what happened to me, and I promise you it's the truth, or my name isn't Mr. B. Bear.

2   Long ago, back when I was young, I had a long bushy tail. I was extremely proud of my tail, which was better-looking than any other bear's, if I do say so myself.

3   One bitter winter day I was lumbering along when I ran into Ms. Fox, who just happened to be carrying a whole mess of freshly-caught fish. "Oh, Ms. Fox, ma'am," I said, "please tell me where you got that delicious-looking set of fish."

4   "Why, certainly, Mr. Bear," said Ms. Fox politely, and she gestured toward the north. "If you walk that way," she told me, "you'll see a beautiful lake. Walk out on the ice and find a hole just big enough for your tail. Coat your tail with honey and dip it down into the water. The fish will grab onto your tail and get stuck. Just haul your tail back up when you think you have all the fish you need."

5   "Thank you very much, ma'am," I said.

6   Well, I found the lake just fine. I walked out on the ice, found a hole, and coated my tail with honey. Then I stuck my tail down the hole and sat. Within five minutes I could tell that at least a dozen fish were stuck to my tail. I started to get up, but changed my mind. If a dozen fish were good, then two dozen fish would be better.

7   So I waited till I was pretty sure I had two dozen fish. Then I decided to wait till there were three dozen. Finally, after four dozen fish, my tail was getting awfully cold. So I stood up. Only I couldn't. My tail was stuck tight in the icy clutches of the lake!

8   I began to panic. I couldn't stay there forever! So I gave one mighty heave, and my body got up all right, but my tail stayed right where it was, frozen solid in the ice!

9   And so that's why bears have short stubby tails these days. And that's the truth, or my name isn't Mr. B. Bear!

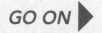
GO ON

Name _____ Date _____

3 How do the different points of view make the stories different?

_____

_____

_____

_____

_____

4 Complete the T Map diagram. Explain how the plots of the two stories are alike and how they are different.

How Stories are Alike	How Stories are Different

Explain how the details in the chart compare and contrast the stories.

_____

_____

_____

_____